Did I Say That Out Loud?

Did I Say That Out Loud?

Musings from a Questioning Soul

Meg Barnhouse

Skinner House Books
Boston

Published by Skinner House Books, an imprint of the Unitarian
Universalist Association of Congregations, a liberal religious
organization with more than 1,000 congregations in the U. S. and
Canada. 25 Beacon St., Boston, MA 02108-2800.

Printed in the United States

Cover design by Kimberly Glyder
Author photos by Susan M. Newton

ISBN 978-1-55896-509-6
eBook version: 978-1-55896-589-8

13 12 11 10 / 5 4 3 2

Library of Congress Cataloging-in-Publication Data

Barnhouse, Meg.
  Did I say that out loud? : musings from a questioning soul / Meg
Barnhouse.
      p. cm.
  ISBN-13: 978-1-55896-509-6 (pbk. : alk. paper)
  ISBN-10: 1-55896-509-2 (pbk. : alk. paper) 1. Christian
life—Unitarian Universalist authors. I. Title.
BX9941.3.B37 2006
248.4'891—dc22
                                      2006011561

We gratefully acknowledge permission to reprint the following material:
Excerpt from "The Swan," from *Selected Poems of Rainer Maria
Rilke: A Translation from the German and Commentary by Robert
Bly,* copyright © 1981 by Robert Bly. Reprinted by permission of
Harper Collins Publishers.
Excerpt from "Natural Resources." Copyright © 2002 by Adrienne
Rich. Copyright © 1978 by W. W. Norton Company, Inc., from *The
Fact of a Doorframe: Selected Poems 1950-2001* by Adrienne Rich.
Used by permission of the author and W. W. Norton Company, Inc.

Contents

Foreword

Meg Barnhouse and I met over the phone. About two minutes went by before I realized that I was in the hands of a powerful storyteller. She had me laughing, thinking, and seeing things from a different point of view.

Read this book and you'll be similarly delighted. Meg Barnhouse is a hilarious and brilliant thinker, writer, preacher, and singer. She is someone who might just be touching the most sacred energy vibrating in the universe.

You think I'm playing with you. I'm not.

She's a self-effacing comic genius. She can make fun of herself in circular patterns that fall one upon another like hedgerows in a maze or swirls of clouds in a tornado. She sneaks up on you, because you think she is only trying to get you to laugh at the absurdity of everyday life.

But she's not.

Meg Barnhouse is a fanatical missionary who wants you to march to the lockstep of her vision while knowing perfectly well that you will not, and she gives you the freedom to do what you damn well please. In fact, at times that is what she is begging you to do. She actually believes you might become the perfected saint of the holy and high way, if only you would do what you damn well please.

Her writing is a tad ironic.

But it is never glib. You would never catch her casting the casual aside, unless she thought that might make you listen to her. She pretends to be skeptical in the brazen hope that she can hide her deep and passionate yearning for a little more love, a little more fun, a little more justice, a little better world.

I am begging you not to simply read this book. Please consider memorizing it and reciting long passages at family gatherings. Better yet, buy multiple copies and give them away to strangers in the grocery store parking lot. Clasp the book in both hands and squeeze it until your knuckles turn white. Become tearful and utter in a choked voice, "You must read this book."

This, of course, will not work with teenagers. Tell your teenagers you will ground them if they read this book, and then leave it lying around.

Meg Barnhouse has a number of dead ancestors who tried to ease the world's suffering. Some of them did alright. Others failed miserably. Most probably fell somewhere in the middle. My personal theology is that these dead people live in a land beyond the river that they call the "sweet forever." I believe they watch over us all—you, me, Meg Barnhouse, everybody. They watch people reading about goats in pick-up trucks or silkworms listening to classical music. They watch as these readers giggle and groan with pleasure. I think they turn to each other and smile their most satisfied smiles. Sometimes they cheer.

That's my story and I'm sticking to it.

Pat Jobe

The Stretcher and the Swan

I drove by an accident the other day. Emergency services people were putting a woman on a stretcher. They were tender, attentive, capable. She was being taken care of. Traffic was directed competently around the wreck. It would be cleaned up, hauled away. Taken care of. A fire truck was parked beside the ambulance, its chunky lights flashing. Standing by, just in case a fire happened. So they could take care of it. That was one well-taken-care-of situation.

I wanted to be on that stretcher. I wanted calm and capable people to take care of everything. It looked restful.

I was tired. I was the kind of tired you get at the end of a month-long project. I had pushed through to the finish and I'd made seven mistakes along the way but the thing was done. I was the kind of tired you get when you have ten different people feeling in their heart that you should have done it differently. Their way. I was the kind of tired you get when your house is messy, your grass is too long, your car is cluttered and your gas tank is empty, along with your bank account. A tiny piece of me thought it would be restful to lie down on clean sheets, be fussed over in a clean hospital room, have people bring Jell-o and chicken broth and straws that bend.

Usually I think it's a good day when I don't have to take a ride in an ambulance, and I got back to that state of mind pretty fast. Anyway, I talked to a friend of mine who used to work in an emergency room and she said that what happens when you come in is that fast-moving people with big scissors cut off all your clothes. That didn't sound restful at all. She suggested I pay for a day at a spa where helpful, calm people would fuss over me all day long. I'd rest, but no one would cut off my clothes with scissors. It would be cheaper than a hospital stay, and I could drive home afterward.

I know now that when I have a "stretcher day," when being helpless looks good to me, I just need to rest. How did I get to be a grown-up and not know that I need to rest sometimes? Resting used to sound weak to me. I used to work sick. Well, I still do that.

I used to have two speeds, a hundred miles an hour and full stop. Crash. I thought I was supposed to go and go at full speed until I couldn't go any longer, then I slept. Then I'd wake up and start again.

As I get older I'm adding more gears. I have "slow" now. Some days.

One of my holy books, the *I Ching*, talks about the wisdom of not doing. I get tired when I forget and act like I'm the source of my energy, my love, my creativity. I'm the one who sustains my friends, who gets things done, who works things out.

The poet Rilke wrote about a swan and how awkwardly he moves on the ground. His bearing changes once he lowers himself into the water, which "flows joyfully" beneath him,

while the swan, unmoving and marvelously calm,
is pleased to be carried, each moment more fully grown,
more like a king, further and further on.

I'm experimenting with letting go, allowing wave after
wave to hold me up, move me along.

May I be granted the wisdom to know when to paddle my
feet.

Waist-Deep in the Lake

⌣

Standing in water up to my hips, I was trying to catch minnows. Schools of them flashed by, hundreds of them, silver and blue, looking like stitches of embroidery thread in the water. I should have been able to cup my palm and bring out a handful, but I was having no success. My mother was sitting with her legs stretched in front of her on the gravelly beach. I remember her in khaki shorts and a white shirt, her black hair blowing over her face as she squinted at me and my little sister.

She was more and more unhappy as the days passed. We had come to Lake Geneva about a month before for my father's job. When he went back to the States, we stayed to have a European adventure. When he left, we had to move out of the Hotel Des Bergues, where we were staying on his expense account. We loved the hotel, an elegant brown stone building, its window boxes spilling over with ivy and red geraniums. If we put a pair of shoes in the hall at bedtime, in the morning they would be polished.

Our new lodgings were a couple of rooms in a water-stained pension owned by a sour woman and her silent husband. Mama didn't like it there, but we didn't look for someplace else. We spent nearly every day at the lake. My father wanted us to play with Swiss children and learn French, but the Swiss kids were unfriendly. Mostly we stood in the water, squishing the coarse sand between our toes and trying to catch fish. I felt watchful. My mother was sad and I wasn't sure why.

Children are different in how aware they are of their parents. Mine didn't rage, terrorize me, or hurt me; my survival did not require vigilance about their moods. I was aware of their emotional lives as I would be of tankers passing on the horizon, of interesting large birds flying overhead. I knew my mother was sad but I didn't feel that I could do anything about it. One day she started muttering about my father leaving us behind. A few days later we were on a boat back to the States.

My mother died from breast cancer when I was twenty-three. By then she had come into more of her own. By the time I was fifteen, she was taking us to Europe every summer, driving a VW camper with my sister and me and a friend or a cousin. She had no plan, no reservations, no fear. Sometimes anger can make people grow; it can goad or wake a person up. I think hers worked like that. She showed my father she could have a European adventure. More than that, she showed herself.

I wish I could ask her about it. This year I am forty-nine, as old as she was when she died. Maybe now I can know her in a way I couldn't before.

Memories dart around me as I wade into the past, flashing just under the surface. I'm going to stand here for a while, be still, cup my hands and see what happens.

Speaking to the Locks

Our locks tell us a lot about our lives. Locks of all kinds hold my attention because of a dream I had when I was thirteen. In the dream a gray-haired woman in a white coat sat behind a desk. I knew she was me, far in the future. Behind her on the wall was a cross-stitched sampler with a motto. I wish to this day that I could remember what it said. The words were the most beautiful I had ever heard or read. I was moved, lifted by the beauty of the message. In another dream, I saw a photograph of the same woman in a newspaper clipping. The caption below her picture is all I remember. In bold type, it read, "Speaking to the Locks."

I woke up knowing what I was supposed to do with my life. I was going to "speak to the locks." The phrase has been my guide over the years. Its meaning continues to become clearer as the years go by.

At a party once, I was telling a friend about Ike's, a restaurant in a neighborhood by the railroad tracks. Ike's serves the best chili cheeseburger in the state. From the outside it looks like a dive. But inside you might see the mayor, construction work crews, college professors, and bikers with jailhouse tattoos. You would also see black, white, and Hispanic people, a mix you don't see many places around here.

My friend jumped in: "I know just where that neighborhood is! My mother used to make us lock the car doors when we drove through there, and she would step on the gas to get through fast." He grinned. "We were supposed to lock the doors by sneaking our finger up to the button and pressing it down gently so it didn't make noise. My sister would lunge across the seat and pound the lock down, and Mama would hiss at her, 'Not that way, you'll hurt their feelings!'"

I think about the new road in the middle of town, a four-lane connector with a fine swooping curve and a great view of downtown. The road's location makes supreme sense, unlike some city projects. A road should have been there all along; it's amazing that no one did it sooner.

The new road barely touches a neighborhood that had a bad reputation in the forties and fifties. I still wouldn't want to walk there alone and drunk at three in the morning, but going through at fifty miles an hour is surely as safe as fifty miles an hour anywhere. I know someone who reaches stealthily to lock the car doors when they turn onto that road. What do people think is going to happen? Some wild-eyed person might charge their rolling car, wrench the door open, and do unspeakable things? Wild-eyed people grab you when your car is stopped, not when it's going full speed.

In my old suburban neighborhood I was street captain one year, which meant I had to go door-to-door collecting dues. I rang the bell, and in a minute I heard locks being unlocked from the inside, sometimes two or three of them.

People cracked open the door enough to look out fearfully with one eye. They watched too much TV. I couldn't figure out why else they would imagine that there were roving gangs of folks out to invade our homes.

My friend Jake lives in a downtown neighborhood that is bad by anyone's standards. He sees a couple of crack houses from his front yard. Yet, he told me that on several occasions, he has gone camping and left the front door open for twenty-four hours.

"Open, like unlocked?" I ask.

"No," he said, "standing wide open. Nothing inside was touched." In Spartanburg County you mostly have to look out for being shot or stabbed by someone in your own family. No one bothers strangers much.

Here is what I'm thinking. We're scared of the wrong things. We lock our car doors and take our kids home to where the guns are. We tell them all about being wary of pedophile strangers, and we forget to tell them about protecting themselves from uncles and cousins. We don't let our neighbors into our lives so there is no one to turn to when we're in trouble. We're scared of people, don't want to know them, and worry that they want to rob or rape us, but we don't want to hurt their feelings.

Isolation is greatly to be feared, but our fears keep us alone. Ignorance is greatly to be feared, but our fears keep us at home, associating only with folks of our same nationality, class, and color. Looking like a fool is greatly to be feared, but our fears keep us silent when we should speak up and make us talk too much when we should be quiet, so we end up looking like fools after all. Our fears keep us from bending, growing, changing in a supple way. Our fears lock us down into a narrowness of experience that sucks the marrow from our bones and leaves us dried-up husks in safe homes with satisfactory retirement funds.

Yeah, we're scared of all the wrong things.

Other People's Things

✿

I was standing in ninety-degree heat on black pavement looking at other people's belongings. It was nothing good, just pitiful junk. Big Bill's U-Store-It was cleaning out the storage units of people who hadn't paid their rent in a while. Big Bill's customers had apparently agreed to pay about a hundred dollars a month to store plastic princess play houses, doll beds, a bent TV antenna, and some limp sheets. The auctioneer brought out a box full of empty CD cases, coat hangers, an old microwave, and a couple of crib mattresses.

"Who will give me five dollars for this lot? Four? Three dollars, two, one?"

None of the people standing around would give a dollar for it. Obviously, most of these people had done this before. They looked at the things matter-of-factly. They were sensible and worldly-wise. Next out of the storage unit was a newer microwave, which someone did buy.

It was hard to stand in the heat this long. I tried leaning against the chain link fence, but tiny ants bit my feet. I maneuvered to a spot with fewer ants. An office chair was next on the block. The stuffing on the seat was sticking out, and a roller was missing on one leg.

"Who would buy something like that?" I wondered. A man bid two dollars for it and sat down.

Dang. That was a good trick. If I ever do this again, I will buy the first chair if I can. I wondered if I would have to take it home or if I could just abandon it where it stood when the auction was over. I wondered how many times that same chair had been sold. The storage place could make some money selling the same chairs over and over.

I had recently reviewed everything I own when I moved. I looked at every questionable piece and thought, "Either I have to keep this forever or at some point I have to get rid of it." Carloads of it went to the thrift store. Some things I kept because they had stories. No one would know but me that the little silvery shoes from India with their up-turned toes reminded me of my grandparents, who were missionaries there, or that I keep a stack of temporary tattoos in the fading hope that I will go to a punk rock show one more time.

At the auction, I wondered how my own belongings would look piled on the pavement. I tried to imagine the story behind some of the things the auctioneer pulled out of the units. Maybe the person who paid to store the ancient microwave had hoped to present it to a college-bound child at some point. Or maybe to a museum. Maybe the owners of the pink plastic princess castle couldn't throw it away because they were hoping to have another child. Maybe the guy kept dusty CD cases and coat hangers because he had an idea for a business where he could use those things.

But life must have moved on, tossing, twisting, and spinning. Sweeping these people away from their past and on toward another hope, another idea. Maybe they realized that what they were hanging onto was not worth the space it was taking up, that the next chapter of life needed to continue less encumbered.

Then, thanks to twenty-five years as a therapist, the stories I imagined became sad. Maybe it was because I was still keeping in mental storage the stories of my former clients' lives. They were full of sorrow, death, and destruction, not doing anyone any good. I hoped my clients had left those things with me and that they weren't carrying those things around by themselves so much any more. I sure didn't need to be carrying them, though. Time to let those things go.

I imagined an emotional baggage sale. Sweating strangers would stand over piles of other people's sorrows and pain. I tossed my old resentments, worn stories of hurt and betrayal, misunderstanding, and missed chances into the pile. The strangers would evaluate with canny eyes, shaking their heads and wondering why anyone in her right mind would give storage space to such detritus.

I pictured walking away from that baggage, leaving it there on the hot asphalt. Time to go home. Lighter.

Paddling, No Water

I have learned some things about life from canoes. I'm not saying I know how to paddle. I have been in canoes twice, and both have been learning experiences. The second time was fun.

The first time, a friend and I decided to take one out on a lake. We slid the canoe into the water. She hopped in. I put one foot on the ladder from the dock and one foot into the canoe, holding on to the dock like a sensible person. The canoe tipped over, threw her out, filled with water, and sank to the bottom, about four feet under the water. She pulled herself back up onto the dock, dripping. I was still hanging on to the ladder.

From this I learn that there are some situations in life where it is dumb to be cautious. You just have to let go, put your whole self in instead of hedging your bets. The trick is to figure out when you are in such a situation, because often it's smart to be cautious.

I took hold of the rope at the front of the canoe, still attached to the dock, and heaved the thing up out of the water. The canoe was heavy, and I was in my mid-forties at the time. Did I ask for help? No. Did I get the canoe back up onto the deck? Yes, in one heave. Did I hurt myself? You bet. Torn rotator cuff. It's gotten lots better, but I use the twinges it still gives me to remind myself to ask for help.

The next time—the fun time—I was on the river in Virginia at a canoe workshop, where the whole purpose was to teach people how to paddle. Nothing but my pride got hurt this time.

Here is what happened. The river was low because of a drought that year. Quite low.

We put in at a bend where the river was deep enough for us to paddle around in pairs. I got instructions on the proper way to get into a canoe, the motion of the paddle, the knack of coordinating with my paddling partner, the rhythm and glide.

For a couple of hours we paddled in pairs, and then it was time for solo work. By this time we were downriver a bit. The instructors sat in one canoe. They paddled fast down a stretch of river and then turned sideways to us so they could help us by shouting suggestions. I didn't know where the others were (back up the river, I think), but I was trying to get to where the instructors were. The water was so shallow that I couldn't get much pressure with the paddle; it kept slipping through the water or knocking against the rocks on the bottom. "Try paddling faster," they shouted. I stepped it up. The canoe moved maybe a foot forward.

I come from a culture that believes in trying hard. I was taught that success is 10 percent inspiration and 90 percent perspiration. And it's true, of course. Except when it's not. I paddled, fast and furious, on that drought-stricken stretch of river, until I noticed the instructors laughing.

14

"You can get out and just walk it down here to where the water's deeper," they shouted.

Oh.

Sometimes we try too hard or in the wrong way. We push too hard, poke at things too much, take on things that aren't ours, take over when we're not supposed to. I'm going to plan, in my life, not to try so hard in water that's too shallow. I have asked my inner wisdom to throw that picture up on the inner screen when I'm in that kind of situation—working the paddles through that inch and a half of water, hearing the divine instructors, the angel guides, up ahead just guffawing. Yeah, that'll help.

Goat in the Pickup

Some sights in this world embed themselves in memory and encapsulate a truth about life in a way that words just can't. I saw one of those one day when I was driving up Route 64 in the mountains of North Carolina toward the town of Cashiers. I came up fast behind a slow flatbed pickup truck. In the back of the truck was a man holding a goat. The goat was standing, stiff-legged, and the man was talking to it. The goat was trying to look over the side of the truck bed, but the scenery whizzing past was no comfort. The man, who had warm-brown skin and the clothes of a farmer, kept talking in its ear. Slowly the goat folded its legs and sat down in the man's lap. Lifting its head into the breeze, eyes closed, it finally relaxed.

I could almost hear myself with my next therapy client, saying, "Yep, this is a real goat-in-the-back-of-a-pickup-truck situation."

I recognized that situation. I have been a goat in the back of a pickup truck heaving itself around mountainous curves. Out of place, out of my element. Deeply confused, with no helpful experience to help me deal with my predicament. Sometimes there is someone whispering in my ear, "Just stay calm. Sit down, give up. Everything's going to be all right."

In such situations, the first thing I want to do is keep my feet. I want to stay up, ready to spring into action at a moment's notice. I want to see over the side even though that only makes things worse. I can't figure out if I'm on my way to a better place with deeper grass and better company, or whether I'm being transported to the slaughterhouse.

The whole time the voice is saying, "Just sit for a while and relax. Surrender to events. Don't try to intervene at this time. Detach yourself from outcomes."

I don't know whether the voice is from the Spirit of Life or the goat-meat factory. Eventually I figure out that there is nothing to be done at this point. My fear isn't helping. My feet can't help. My alertness is working against me. I need to let go until such time as action is possible.

I decide to enjoy the nice voice in my ear, to sit down to gather my thoughts, to worry about it all later.

I have worked hard to find my place, to find my strength, to surround myself with trusted voices. Every now and then, though, I still find myself in a goat-in-the-pickup-truck situation.

May I be given the wisdom to know when to sit and just let my ears flap in the breeze.

The Greening Breath

∿

My new house has roses blooming all along its sunny southern side. Mama told me roses were hard to grow, so I never tried, but here they are, and I like watching them.

A medieval Christian mystic named Hildegarde of Bingen wrote, "The breath of the air makes the earth fruitful. Thus the air is the soul of the earth, moistening it, greening it."

Watching my roses, I see that greening breath moving up slowly through the stem, sending energy through the tips of the leaves as they uncurl, gathering in what they need from the summer sun. Hildegarde of Bingen said, "The soul is a breath of living spirit, that with sensitivity permeates the entire body to give it life."

I'm wishing for that greening spirit in my soul this summer. The heat drains the life out of me. Some days I drag around, crabby and overwhelmed. I see people on TV having cookouts, rafting down refreshing rivers, enjoying places I can't afford this year. I know that comparing my life to life on TV is a no-win practice. When I'm hot, everyone else seems graceful, loving, patient, financially savvy, organized. They do things a little at a time rather than letting everything pile up. But everything is too hard for me when it's hot, or maybe I'm too soft. I can't tell. The greening is hard for me to feel in summer, but I see my roses feeling it as they bloom.

Sometimes I wonder if it hurts to bloom. I imagine I'm a rose. Do I love being a bud, all curled around myself, feeling hugged and tight, knowing what's what? I soak up the sun, I am gently tossed in warm wind, and suddenly everything starts to loosen up. My petals are letting go! They are moving apart from one another! Do I try to hold on, grab for the edges, and keep the changes from happening? Perhaps I think, "I don't understand this, but maybe it's what's supposed to happen."

I allow the once tight petals to move apart. Does it hurt? Does it cause anxiety? Do I think I'm falling apart or do I realize that I'm blossoming?

The roses seem to accept each stage with grace, but how do we really know? Maybe we just can't hear them screaming.

I'm going to try to trust, imagining that whatever is happening is supposed to happen. Maybe this faith is well founded or maybe it's not, but I'm going to try it out for a while. The shoot, the stem, the flower, then the seed, all in their own time.

I'm just musing, watching these roses. Surrendering to summer. May the greening seep into my soul.

Centers of the Universe

∵

The place where my writer friends regularly meet for coffee in the morning always closes for the week of July Fourth. The whole South goes on vacation. Industry shuts down. If you are not at Myrtle Beach eating fried popcorn shrimp at an all-you-can-eat buffet or playing putt-putt, you are so far out of the mainstream that you have to hunker down, fighting to keep whatever semblance of routine you can scrape together. The writers made an alternative plan for morning coffee and conversation, sitting hungrily around tables in a new place where they don't have food until lunch time. We call the regular coffee shop "The Center of the Universe." We didn't choose this name out of arrogance. The coffee shop is, for us, the vortex of conversation and friendship. I don't think we will call this alternate place "The Center of the Universe" as if the center moves with us. It doesn't. The other place has too much history, too many tears, jokes, angry exchanges later forgiven, loving support given with the lightest touch.

We know, of course, that it is not the center of the universe for anyone else. It seems obvious to me that the Universe has many centers. I'm not sure how that would make sense in the world of physics, although I bet it could. I know how it makes sense in the world of thought and feeling. You get attached to a place. Even when the new owners put a giant and noisy ice maker right beside the tables where we usually gather, it took us months to come up with the idea of moving to a different set of tables further from the grinding and clunking.

A young woman walked by us a couple of weeks ago and said, "Are you all still here?" Apparently she had left town for a few years. Now she was back. We were there when she left, and we were still there when she came back.

I felt ashamed to be there after all those years. I wanted to say, "Uh, I'm just back visiting. I've been in, uh, Peru! Yeah, in Peru, leading a movement for fairer treatment of, uh, coffee bean pickers."

I haven't, though. I've been here. The whole time. Living life. In this place. Raising children. Doing work. Thinking about things and writing down my thoughts. I never imagined I would be in this one place so long. I have been other places; I've traveled around the world from here.

Why did I feel shamed by that young woman for being still here, as if I should have been a war correspondent, flying off to a different place every few weeks, each more dangerous than the last?

Surely we make our lives wherever we are. We make our homes the best we can, we do work that supports our families and if we're lucky, it supports our souls too. We make a community to belong to, we learn to be friends, we accumulate a history.

Where else should I be? What should I be doing by now?

I sometimes wish I lived in Toronto, where the winters drive folks indoors to cafes and theaters, where the coffee is strong and you listen to musicians down in the subway stations. I would love to live in San Francisco in a loft with windows high in the ceiling, concrete floors and brick walls, a bakery downstairs, people walking by at all hours of the day and night, where everything doesn't shut down the week of the Fourth of July.

For right now, though, this is my life—in a house so lovely I shuffle out of the bedroom every morning and think, "I can't believe this is my house." I have built a family here in the South, in this small town. It only has one tall building, but I have friends here whom I adore. What would I do in a big city but try to recreate what I already have here? Could I replace the people who are so dear to me? I would have to make a new garden. I don't want to start over again. Is this why people stay put?

How do I find a balance between roots and risk? Routine and revolution? Is there an option in between filming segments on the latest car bombing as a sandstorm whips my hair into my face and being caught in the gravity of one place so firmly that it becomes impossible to pull free, even when it's time?

I'll keep you posted.

Brick by Brick

✎

All summer, workers have been building a brick wall along the road by my neighborhood. Against the brutal heat, they stretch a tarp overhead to get a little shade. I've watched them take bricks in their dusty brown hands one by one, butter them thickly with mortar, line them up, and tap them down—row by row. One man who looks to be in his seventies is the leader. His skin is the color of bittersweet chocolate; his beard is gray. Slender and tall, he moves from one group of bricklayers to the next, reaching and bending, looking like a heron in a marsh. When he pauses, he stands very straight. I see him teach the others how to do the work.

He stoops over to look at a line of bricks, hands on his thighs, inspecting the work. Sometimes as I drive by, I see him put his hand on the back of the person he's teaching. Often they are both smiling.

He looks like he loves what he's doing. I wonder how he can love building walls, day after day, handling bricks, teaching the art of laying bricks. Is it the teaching he loves? Seeing how his students learn, what their styles are, how their work shows their character? Does he love the wall itself? Does he know about when it'll be done? Does he look forward to seeing it finished? Or does he love the process, the feel of the bricks in his hands, the squish of the mortar, the challenge of making the symmetry of pillars and arches, the geometry of it?

I think, from the look on his face, that he loves the process. I imagine that he never thinks about the end of the project, the completion of the wall. I think he will go on to the next wall as if it were just a continuation of this one, then the next one and the next, and never be bored.

I want to be like that, and I am, I guess. In my job as a minister, the bricks are stories. I hear stories of family and work, stories of loss and reconciliation, stories of rejection and disaster, illness and healing, birthing and dying. I tell stories every Sunday and in between, teaching, challenging, confessing, inviting people to learn and laugh and think.

Brick by brick, story by story, we build a church, seeing the patterns, the symmetry, the plain joy of setting one story on the other, sustained by the strong and beautiful structures they make. We will never be finished.

It's okay.

Dervishes

I remember the Sufi dancers I saw in a dark mosque in Istanbul. We'd followed our guide down narrow streets, turning corners that never made right angles. Slipping through a battered green door that looked like it led no place special, we fell quiet looking at pillars, high windows, and a domed ceiling. We took our seats on wooden folding chairs set up behind the pillars, where we could be hidden in the shadows. The dancers could pretend we weren't there, watching their worship. A shaft of sunlight slanted through a window high above, and motes of dust floated through it as our breath moved the still air.

Our guide, sitting in front of us, muttered over his shoulder, "These men are forbidden to practice their dervish dancing in Turkey these days unless they do it for tourists, which is the reason they have agreed to do it today. Please be respectful, as this is their only chance to pray."

Nine men filed in silently and took their places in a circle. They wore white outfits, *tennures*, with full sleeves and long skirts, red fez hats on their heads. I don't remember any music. Maybe there was some. What I remember is the Dervishes, these Muslim mystics who seek an experience with the Beloved Divine, raising one arm, palm up toward heaven, extending the other palm down toward the earth. Slowly they began to spin. The hems of their robes swirled and lifted. Their skirts twirled slightly, circling as the dancers went around. Their faces, raised toward the light, were solemn, enraptured. They didn't "spot," as dancers do, to avoid dizziness. Faces and bodies spun together.

Then they stopped. Together they all stopped. They didn't stagger or wobble. They stood still, slowly dropped their arms, and bowed. They raised their arms again and began to spin in the opposite direction.

Watching, I was in as much of a trance as they were. This wasn't only an amazing tourist experience, it was religion, theirs and mine. I was awed by their focus, their devotion. I felt the Spirit move them and me as I watched. Their faces were not ethereal faces of angelic beings, but the faces of young and older men who worked in car garages and textile warehouses, rough faces you could see in any tea shop on the street arguing over politics or the best way to run a soccer team. The whole person behind each face was utterly given over to the Spirit for the duration of this dance. They prayed in their beloved community as they danced together across the bare wooden floor.

Of course I tried it later. It was difficult to spin and stop, then spin the other way, but I discovered that as I spun, I found a still place inside. That still place isn't dizzy. I don't know how it works. It is the same still place I can get to through yoga or meditation, in prayer or sitting by a creek. It's that place where I have a glimpse of what it feels like to be held in the arms of love, to be grounded in the Great Compassion, to be washed in light and encompassed by sacred dark.

As I recall those mystics spinning between earth and heaven, through the shaft of sunlight and back into the dimness of the room, the memory feeds me. Their crimson hats, their raptured faces live in my soul. I am eternally grateful to have been present at their prayers. They are always present at mine.

Dumpster Pumpkins

A tall man with white hair stands in a dumpster looking through the trash. Two women stand on the street offering encouragement and appreciation. To tell the complete truth, we are also laughing. Here is how this happened:

Steve, the handsome, white-haired man, volunteers his time and energy to clean our church. His main field of expertise is applied mathematics, but cleaning makes him hum and whistle. He was putting the building back in order after our Halloween festival. We had spider races, a spells-and-potions room, a spooky surgery room, a fortune-teller, and a pumpkin-decorating contest. Steve and I were standing in the building's foyer talking companionably when Kris, our director of religious education, who rarely moves slowly, dashed up the hall from her office, spun around in the foyer, and said, "Where are the pumpkins that were down there?" She pointed at the empty floor.

"Oh, I threw those away." Steve said.

"Where are they?"

"Out in the dumpster," Steve answered.

Kris looked stricken. "I promised the kids they could pick up their pumpkins Sunday after the paint dried. It was a promise."

"Let's get them," was Steve's instant reply.

Kris is a good mother. Steve is a good grandfather. They understand that a promise made to a child has to be kept. The three of us trooped off to the dumpster. Kris carried a box for the pumpkins. Steve carried the ladder. Setting it against the side of the dumpster, he climbed up and jumped in. He looked around.

"I wonder how I'm going to get out?" he mused aloud.

Picking around in the garbage for the pumpkins, Steve placed each one carefully in the box Kris lifted up to him. They counted, and when all the pumpkins had been rescued, Steve muscled himself onto the side of the dumpster and jumped to the ground. We clapped and whistled. I would be glad to know one person who would dumpster-dive to keep a promise to a child. I know at least two.

Had I been by myself, I don't know if I would have been that ready to dive for the kids' sake. I might have been more ready to tell them I was sorry, the pumpkins were thrown away by accident, and they would just have to deal. I would have been sensible about it. That jump into the dumpster isn't in my makeup. I think I wish it were. I would prefer to be one of those people from whom the kids learn to make enormous efforts to keep their promises rather than one of those people from whom they learn to deal with disappointment.

I don't trust the world enough to make promises. Telling my children about something I want to do for them, I always try to say, "That's my intention and my plan, but it's not a promise, because you never know what will happen."

I know Kris and Steve, having lived more than thirty years each on this earth, have as much reason to mistrust the world as I do. Yet they make promises.

Maybe it's not only the world that I don't trust. Maybe I don't trust my own strength or resolve. I broke those first wedding vows, in which I promised at twenty-three to love the man for the rest of my life. So much wrath, so much guilt followed the breaking of those promises that I decided never to make one again. After all, look where it gets you: knee deep in garbage, wondering how you're going to get out.

Steve did get out, though, and Kris's promise to the children was kept. It wasn't that hard. It was even fun. My desire to stay clean by never making another promise suddenly strikes me as emotionally prissy. I don't want to be prissy in any way. Maybe I will start small, with little promises, and see what happens.

If I end up in the dumpster, you can stand in the street and laugh at me. I hope I'll be laughing too.

Disaster Season

Recently, while enduring a long run of unpleasant life experiences, I had the idea to name them like the weather service names hurricanes. It might provide a dose of realism, of preparedness, to come up with an alphabetical list of names at the beginning of the year, acknowledging that disaster season does come around, even into blessed and lucky lives.

I have had a fairly mild disaster season this year so far. Last week I had a dentist appointment to get a crown on one of my back teeth. I complained of a little swelling under the tooth, so they took an X ray, "just to be on the safe side."

The screen in my mind showed a possible disaster brewing, way out to sea. Call her "Ava."

Sure enough, the X ray showed trouble. The tooth was infected. Infected and dying. They could save it with a root canal. Did they do root canals where I was? Nope. I had to go to someone else's office. The dentist's office manager called and got me an appointment for that very same day for my first root canal.

"It won't hurt much," the office manager said, "it's like a filling."

Stifling a sigh, I went to the parking lot to get on with it.

Dropping into the seat of my car, putting my head back to gather my courage and good character, I rested for a moment before venturing on to the endodontist's office. When I felt ready to go, I turned the key in the ignition. Nothing happened. Not even a click.

Unbidden, the name "Bruce" came to me. Disaster Bruce was hard on the heels of disaster Ava.

I called my friend Pat, who came to get me. I called my trusty mechanic, Charlie, who said, "Leave it to me." By that he meant he would call a tow truck, have my car delivered to his shop, fix what was wrong, and call me when it was ready. In disaster season, it is of the utmost importance to have this kind of support system already in place. We all know that once in a while it can get really bad. Don't wait until the middle of the storm to make friends and gather trustworthy helpers. Crates of water and bags of provisions must be in place. Butter cream mints are not a bad idea either.

Pat delivered me to the office where I had my root canal. On the way there, he provided comfort and joy. The office manager had been right. The root canal was not a big deal. I usually ask for gas when I'm getting a filling, but I went through this root canal stone sober. I was numbed with Novocaine of course, but my consciousness was unaltered. Charlie picked me up afterward and drove me to my car, which he had fixed while I was getting patched up.

A day or so ago, my beloved and I had a misunderstanding. Okay, it was a fight. That added disaster "Clarice" to the count. We talked it through, though, with great understanding and emotional maturity, 80 percent of which was not mine. I hope it's a little while before "Daniel" comes along.

Taking my cue from the weather people, I'm wondering whether to name all the disasters I might see coming, far out on the horizon off the coast of some karmic Africa. But Mark Twain was right when he said, "I have dealt with a lot of problems in my life, some of which actually happened." Disasters often fizzle out over the wideness of the water or they blow out to sea.

I could follow the weather people's lead and call these potential disasters "tropical depressions." That's a colorful phrase. I've seen depressions before, but they weren't particularly tropical. They felt more cold and dark, not much fun at all. Tropical ones sound much more festive.

When I see a potential disaster on the horizon, I plan to gather my friends around, have my trusty helpers' phone numbers close at hand, sip fruity rum drinks with umbrellas in them, dance to Cuban music, and keep half an eye on the weather channel.

A Walk in Winter

⁖

Walking toward the beach on a cold winter day under
the rustling palmettos and the pine trees with their long,
soft-looking needles shimmering in the wind, I see a small
dog standing on the wooden path that crosses the dunes.
Elderly and dignified, he is cognac-colored, part chow.
Despite his tattered coat his eyes are calm and bright. He
seems to be waiting for me. As he trots on ahead, I wonder
whether he wants to lead me somewhere, perhaps to his
fallen master. Thinking this might lead to reporting a dead
body, I check my cell phone to see if it has a signal.

When I catch sight of the water, I realize my mistake
instantly. My murder-mystery-reading, TV-watching mind
clears in the face of the wide sand, the glittering immensity
of ocean, the inverted blue bowl of sky over us. The dog
is just glad to have a walking companion. His ears flap as
he trots along, his short legs working fast to stay ahead of
me. Those ears seem so dear, they make me smile. I think
about my usual words as I lead my congregation into the
time of meditation and prayer, "Now is the time for prayer
and meditation, to pray to God as you understand God,
to listen for the Wisdom that is inside us, to breathe on
that spark of the Divine that, as Unitarian Universalists, we
believe lives in the soul of every being."

The theological questioner in my head asks, "Are you sure
you want to say 'every being' instead of 'every person'? Do

you really think that there is a spark of the Divine in that dog there?"

Still smiling about his ears flapping in time with his trot, I think that I have absolutely no trouble seeing God in that dog up there.

"So everything that has Being has God?" the questioner asks.

I sense a trick coming. Does an ugly animal have God in it? Yes. A dangerous animal? An alligator? Yes. A mole? Yes. "A cancer cell?" it asks.

Maybe yes. Cancer could be a kindness, the universe's gardener pulling up plants so that others can have room to grow. The thought is hard to swallow.

My younger son once read a poem to me, a Stephen Crane poem in which the refrain says, "War is kind." I told him I was sure Crane was being sarcastic, but maybe if I could get to the place where I see cancer as the hand of a benevolent force working for the good of the entire universe, I might be a more peaceful person. Would I be a wiser person, though, or a peaceful fool?

Maybe if I could see war as kind, see that there are some people "born to drill and die," as Crane says, I could be less anguished. My heart wouldn't wail about all the young men and women suffering and dying. The mind of a mother of sons, though, is never far from the specter of her own boys being killed in a war. I work hard to keep my mind from being lured to that dark place, but I remembered Crane's poem talks about a "mother's heart, humble as a button sewn onto the shroud of her son. . . ."

Tears spill from my eyes. How did I get here, from minding my own business on a walk with a dog to this pain in my heart, this fear and worry?

I mentally shake myself to break the spell. War is not kind, war is stupid. A cancer cell doesn't have God in it, not to my way of thinking, not yet. Just because something has being doesn't mean it's a being, and that's where I'm going to draw the line in seeing God.

I steer my attention away from the possibility of my sons' death in a war and back to the rustling pines, the singing blue of the Carolina sky, the dignified dog who is walking with me. Beauty doesn't prove a benevolent Spirit behind the universe, any more than ugliness and cruelty disprove it. The possibility of death cannot be allowed to make life an exercise in despair. On this winter day on the coast, beauty is now, and my sons are healthy and alive, and my heart is with those who suffer, but I am not suffering here in this moment, and this moment is all I have. The dog and I fling our praises into the same sky, and the sun feels good on our backs.

Bread, Not Stone

Ↄ

I parked by the side door of the church of my childhood. All grown up now, I walked through the door marked "Church Office." I was here to baptize my cousin's daughter, Emma. My footsteps on the speckled linoleum echoed off the bare hallway walls.

Usually someone greets the visiting minister, to show her around and give her a room where she can put on her robe. This person might tell her how to get to the sanctuary, maybe introduce her to the other people with whom she will be working. There was no such person to greet me in this place.

It smelled the same, a combination of old hymnbooks and institutional disinfectant. Mustiness and astringency in an ongoing struggle, the Yin and Yang of my Protestant church life. Mama, my sister, and I came to this church Sundays and Wednesdays until I was ten. Memories rose like ground fog: Sunday school classes, sitting through long sermons, going back to church Sunday evening for a service called "Vespers," seeing my mother struggle to fit her life to the dogma, watching for that tight smile of concern on a teacher's face when a child asked or said something surprising.

This ethnic Scottish denomination does not allow women to be ministers. Women are not even allowed to be deacons, the first level of leaders who serve in the congregation by visiting members and being on committees. My cousin had been brave to ask me to baptize her baby here. I had been brave to accept. A weight of dread was gathering in my chest and on my shoulders. A part of me was sliding back into being ten years old again.

In an office down the hall, a pale gray man in a gray suit sat at a desk shuffling some papers. I knocked on the half-open door.

"I'm Meg Barnhouse. I'm here for Emma's baptism."

He nodded slightly and gave me a pinched smile. He rose and shook my hand, introducing himself as the assistant minister. Without coming around the desk, nodding at a closed door to his left, he said, "That's the minister's office." He smiled again, not in a nice way. "I guess you could use the sitting room across the hall." He sat back down again and bent his head to his papers.

I had to remind myself to stand up tall as I crossed the hall alone to find the sitting room. Its walls were painted peach and there was a heavy mirror over a mantel. White French Provincial furniture was placed tastefully around the room. Curtains printed with big flowers hung at the windows. I considered what it would do to my relationship with my cousin if I were to turn around and drive the two and a half hours back home right now. Why stay in a place where they feel contempt for me? Why act as if I believe in a God who does not believe in me?

I had arrived too early; no one from my family was around. I alternated between hanging around in the sitting room, which felt like hiding, and wandering the halls. Finally I heard someone coming. When he rounded the corner, I saw my cousin Jimmy. I caught hold of him like a lifeline and held on until the rest of the family got there.

Nothing had changed in thirty years. In the sanctuary, the pews were painted white, the carpet was the same red I remembered, the tall plain glass windows were still covered with white louvered shutters. The racks on the backs of the pew held hymnbooks, hardback Bibles, visitor cards, and the stub of a pencil. There were two holes in which to place the tiny communion cups once you've drunk the grape juice during the quarterly Communion. My old Sunday school teacher introduced herself sweetly, looking exactly the same as she had looked when I was in her class.

It was both a fierce joy and a grinding ordeal to be a minister in this familiar place. I was grateful to my cousin for bringing me back to this place that deeply resisted all of who I was and what I stood for. It felt like she had enlisted me as an ally in a battle for change. I was honored by her request. At the same time I hated baptizing Emma, one of the most beautiful babies I'd ever laid eyes on, into this church that was going to tell her lies about girls and their place in the world. Maybe my cousin wouldn't bring her here for very long.

Driving home, I squinted against the setting sun which pierced my eyes like a nail driven by an implacable hand. On the highway, I could only see the middle of the road. My head felt like it might split in two. I had only heard about migraine headaches before, but I was pretty sure this was one. It came to me that I was about to throw up. I pulled into a mini-mart to get to a bathroom, but I didn't get the car door open fast enough. I puked all over the door, all over my clothes.

The young woman behind the counter gave me a roll of paper towels and some water to clean up with. After leaning the car seat back and sleeping there in the parking lot for a while, I gingerly steered back onto the interstate.

I thought about my cousin, trying to change that church from the inside. I thought about Emma, growing up there, asking for the truth, looking for the love in what was told to her.

Rabbi Jesus asked, "Is there any one among you who, if your child asks for bread, will give a stone?"

I broke my teeth on so much of what I heard in church growing up. I managed to take it in, thinking there was something wrong with me for not finding nourishment in it. What I couldn't take in was lovingly and repeatedly put in my mouth, with cheery yummy noises, little bits of stone that became a misery inside.

Those people all tried to do the right thing. Those people earnestly tried to teach what they thought God wanted us to believe about men being leaders and teachers while women are only meant to teach children and other women, cook food for church dinners and grieving families, and discuss things among themselves.

I still don't let myself know how much anger and hurt I carry for the lies, lovingly told to us, for all the girl-souls, lovingly bound to stay small, while the voices whispered, "These bindings will make you more lovely, more pleasing to the Lord, more sweetly useful, more willing to stay in the place that has been made for you."

Almost home, I had to pull over and throw up again.

A friend later muttered, "Kryptonite. That's what it is to you." It's not, though. It's just stone.

If I Were the Devil

I could try to pretend to be discouraged, but I'm not. I'm distressed. I want to say disgusted, but I'm really just mad.

I want to go all prophetic on some of my fellow church folks. The Jewish prophets railed against the empty celebrations on which the people insisted. They called the people back to faithfulness with mockery, imagery, ranting, and preaching. I feel like taking a page out of the prophet book this year. Here's why.

It will soon be Christmas and all over the United States, big churches are spending their energy organizing boycotts of businesses where people say, "Happy Holidays" instead of "Merry Christmas."

These churches are not organizing against the commercialization of this birthday of Jesus, friend of the poor. They're not organizing food banks. On this birthday of the Prince of Peace, they are not protesting the war we're fighting. What they are doing instead is sending their folks out into the mall to give prune-faced rebukes to hapless workers with sore feet who make the mistake of trying to be pleasant.

The churches say the "Happy Holidays" greeting waters down the impact of Christmas. They say the secular humanists, who are bent on erasing Christmas, have intimidated the merchants. I'm guessing the real reason for the greeting is that many of these merchants feel it's kind to include our non-Christian neighbors in the season's greetings.

One of the members of this movement said, "There are more of us than them," implying that outnumbering a minority means you don't have to consider them. True, odds are that, in this part of the world, the person you are greeting will be Christian, but do these church people want to behave like triumphal bullies, hopped up on righteousness and their majority status? Is that how their preachers want them to behave? I'm not mocking the religion these folks profess. I'm mocking what they are focusing on. They're not even close to practicing their religion in this situation.

I don't believe in a personal devil, but this kind of experience makes me wonder. Let me put it this way. If I were Satan, and I were faced with a burgeoning group of God's people, full of energy and passion, called to feed the poor, preach liberty to the captives, comfort the sorrowful, be peacemakers, I would find a way to stop them.

How?

I would hire myself some preachers. I would instruct them to distract the people, to keep the whole group too busy to do much good for maybe twenty, twenty-one centuries. What would I keep them busy with? Keeping teenagers from having sex before marriage. That should do it. Arguing about homosexuality. "We love them, but we hate their lifestyle. We welcome them into our churches, as long as they don't talk about their lives, their anniversaries, their kids, or their history. We will ordain them as long as they don't love anyone in an intimate way, blah blah blah."

If that's not enough to keep the religious powerhouse from solving the problems of poverty, greed, cruelty, violence, and ignorance, we will occupy them with forcing merchants to say "Merry Christmas" instead of "Happy Holidays."

Here is what I recommend for religious liberals when faced with these people. The next time someone is distracting good church people from feeding the hungry and preaching liberty to the captives by being mean about homosexuality, making teens swear they won't have sex until marriage, or forcing merchants not to say "Happy Holidays," just point your finger at them and shout, in your best prophetic voice, "You are doing the work of Satan!" That should spin the conversation in a whole new direction.

However it goes, you won't be bored.

Silk

I have some kind of disorder when it comes to buying and wrapping presents. Either I get the best, coolest thing ever or I can't find anything that's not dull or run-of-the-mill. Worse than socks.

I get sleepy as I'm wrapping because I know I'm not doing it right. "Right" to me means the best it's ever been done, doing it so well that people will be talking next Christmas about what a wonderful wrapping job I did. I imagine wrapping my gift with cloth that is hand stamped, made from silk from caterpillars that were hand raised, with Vivaldi playing in the background. In comparison with the inner perfectionist to whose standards I hold myself, Martha Stewart is merely adequate.

In the real world, I adopt an attitude of despairing carelessness. Why try when I won't be able to come close? Layered over the despair is a sense of irony. I get it that the present will look and be ordinary, even though my feelings for the recipient are far from ordinary. If I had hand raised the caterpillars to classical music, made the wrapping from their silk, and learned the ancient stamping and knotting techniques that would make my wrapping into a work of art, the present still wouldn't match the love with which I mean to present it.

There would still be something wrong with the knot.

I get the joke that perfection can never happen. I've heard of Chinese artists who deliberately put a tiny imperfection in an elaborately carved jade ball because perfection is an insult to the gods. I would never have to put one in deliberately. I don't think they do either, really. Maybe I will make a bumper sticker just for myself—"Imperfection Happens."

I feel a mix of despair and cheerfulness, both of which are responses to my awareness that the perfection in my imagination can never be attained. So I try to relax and have fun—most of the time.

Despair, irony, cheer. Yeah, that's me.

I also know that I don't care if a present is wrapped perfectly when I am given one, so I bet no one is inspecting my wrapping job. They are busy feeling good that they are loved and cherished, glad that they live in a cocoon of friends and family that holds them, not perfectly, but holds them nevertheless. The tyranny of perfectionism is so heavy when it's unexamined, so easy to shrug off once you look at it full on. Why should I despair? I'm doing well enough. In this world all we have to do is learn to love and be loved. That takes the whole time. Nothing else is important. Maybe my wanting to have a shimmering silk ribbon made from my own caterpillar farm is just a way of distracting myself from love with something easier. My heart makes silk that those I love can wrap themselves in, fall softly into, rub absently across their cheeks. Right now it still has a few rough places, but I'm working on it. Sometimes to Vivaldi. The voice of perfectionism becomes a tinny and distant demand. Why should I despair when I am wrapped in a symphony of silk from the hearts of so many friends? What gifts of love I have been given. What gifts I have still to give.

I smile a silky smile.

Good Fortunes

Some people pick their favorite Chinese restaurants by the Bourbon Chicken. In my family, we do it by the fortune cookies. The other night we tried a new place. The food was fine, and the service was lovely, but when I broke apart the cookie after the meal, I read, "Where there's a will, there's a way."

"Where there's a will, there's a way"? That is one lame fortune. Why not "too many cooks spoil the broth," or "a stitch in time saves nine"? If they are going to call it a "fortune," I should at least get the promise of a thrilling time to come, or a journey with unforeseen results.

If I owned a fortune cookie company, I would make the fortunes evocative, something to excite the imagination, shine a light on new possibilities, so that people's perspectives would shift after their meal. I might put in something like "You will see three beautiful things tomorrow." Then the whole next day, the person would have their eyes open, looking for beauty. They would ask themselves, "What is beauty? Is that tree the beautiful thing? Is my spouse the beautiful thing? This hand of mine? The glimpse of my miraculous eye in the rearview mirror that enables such beauties to pour into my heart?"

Maybe I would write, "Seven people love you madly." What would that make of your next several days? You would look at each of your friends with a secret smile. "Are you one of them? I knew you liked me fine, but do you love me madly?" How about this one: "You will figure something out two days from now" or "They appreciate what you did." Why not? People certainly get slipped awful little messages in innocuous forms. A partner says, "You don't get it," or "You're just like your father." We receive messages from bosses, parents, friends, and from that venomous voice inside that knows all about us and doesn't think much of any of it. Why not interrupt the spread of discouragement and dismissal with a tidbit for the soul after a Chinese meal? I would love to get a fortune that says, "Don't try to improve yourself tomorrow." Tell me that wouldn't make you laugh out loud. What would it do to your perspective if you read, "The next two years are just for fun"?

Here is what I'm going to do. I'm going to write these down just for myself and keep them in a bowl by the bed. I'll draw one out every morning and see what happens to my eyes, to my ears, to my heart and my spirit. Maybe I will pass them around at parties. Join me, and together we can whisper peachy little perspective-shifters into one another's days. I'm looking forward to the twinkle in your eye.

Fighting Clutter

❦

You know it's getting serious when you trip and stub your toe on a book that's lying on the floor in your house. Breathing shallowly through the pain, you pick it up and glance at the title, *Fighting Clutter*. Some people say, "As without, so within," and you are supposed to unclutter your living and working space in order to unclutter your mind.

I picked up a magazine in the grocery checkout line because it promised an article called "150 Cleaning Tips." I opened the magazine to the cleaning tips article and left it in the bathroom for two weeks until I had both the time and the inclination to read it.

"Clean from the top down," it said. Okay, that's helpful, only the tops of things are hard to reach, and they're grimy. Yuck. All that grime slides down on what used to look clean.

"For grease spots behind the stove, rub them with a heavy-duty household cleaner and a plastic scrubbing pad. When the wall is clean, apply a coat of paste wax. Future spots will come off easily."

Wax your walls? This hint must be for people of Scandinavian or Dutch descent, people who live in the Midwest maybe, people who are serious about cleaning. A professor of sociology who taught with me at the college had moved to the South from Wisconsin. At the faculty lunch table one day, she complained about a sore back. When asked, she said she had hurt it moving the refrigerator to clean behind it. We said we hadn't known she was moving to another house. She told us she was not moving, she was just cleaning behind her refrigerator because it was time to do that. The rest of us were astonished. She explained that in Wisconsin, people clean behind their refrigerators even when they are not moving to another house.

Another tip from the magazine said, "Remove the hooks from your drapes and run them through the dryer on a no-heat setting. Throw in a damp towel to attract the dust. Rehang immediately to prevent wrinkling."

Number one, removing the drapes from the windows is something you should only do when moving to a new house. You should never have to take those hooks out and put them back in again, unless you're in prison and a cruel guard is trying to break your spirit.

The article suggested baking soda for a mustard stain. Interesting. Rubbing alcohol removes permanent marker. Good to know. These stain-removing tips are too good to throw away. I wish I could find room to remember them in my brain, but that is a vain hope. Now that magazine is somewhere in the house. In a pile of clutter.

My mother was an indifferent housekeeper. She taught second graders all day and did not have energy for nonessentials. She grew up in India, and her idea of essentials was not the usual for this country. When my father complained about the spiders camped out beside their egg sacs between the window panes and the storm windows, she waved him away.

"It's science!" she caroled, claiming she left them there for educational purposes, so my sister and I could behold the wonders of nature. Mama banned Lysol from the kitchen, calling it poisonous. If some food fell on the floor, she would pick it up, muttering, "Immunities."

I never learned much about cleaning from her, but she and her whole family were good at uncluttering. When something was duplicated or unused, it was given away or thrown out. She came from a family of missionaries, who believed that you should only keep as much as you could carry in a camel caravan or take on a steamship home for furlough.

I'm usually good at throwing things out. When, as a hippie teenager, I asked my mother and grandmother if there were any vintage clothes in the attic. They shrugged, wondering why on earth anyone would keep clothes that were no longer worn instead of passing them along to the next person.

I remember reading somewhere that if you have things you don't use, you are not their rightful owner. Pass them along so the person whose things they were meant to be could find them.

I don't want to hold on to other people's things. If "as without, so within," what does that mean for my mind? A mind filled with other people's ideas that are unusable for me, reactions that don't serve me well, sensitivities that aren't really mine, driving forces that are meant to drive someone else, habits and ways of being that used to be helpful but no longer are. Clearing out that inner clutter is appealing to me.

I have my doubts, though, about whether getting books up off my floor will help with it. It's worth a try, though. At least my toes will thank me.

Floor It, Baby

·.·

The riding mower made a noise I hope never to hear again in my life. I was at the top of the slope, rounding the curve by the street. Suddenly there was a banging and a ringing sound like broadswords in battle. Then a sickening clunk. Then quiet, as the engine died. My heart deflated like a soccer ball the dogs chewed. I tried to lift the mower to see if the blades were okay. It wouldn't budge. The mower was wedged into the grass, stuck tight, run aground. What had I done now? My relationship with the world of things is not good. I called my friends who know about mowers and told them what had happened. They promised to come that evening, which gave me hours in which to berate myself. I mean, I can do other things while I'm berating myself—it doesn't take my whole attention.

That evening my friends unstuck the mower. The engine started up fine. One of them squinted up at me from the mower seat and said, "You were riding this thing wide open, weren't you?" Yes, I had been.

"I like to ride wide open too," the other one said. "This happens to me when I run over small tree trunks."

What is it about some of us that wants to go fast? I had a dream one night that I was dozing in a dark car. I was parked at the top of a steep drop-off thickly planted with trees. Somehow I knocked the gear into neutral and when

I woke up (in the dream) the car was rolling downhill. I steered between the trees, trying not to crash.

When I met with my dream interpretation buddy, she asked me to think about it with my awake mind. What would I do differently if I found myself careening downhill between trees? I thought for a minute. "Um—steer more quickly?"

"That's all you can think of?"

"Y-e-e-e-s." I knew she had something in mind but I couldn't fathom what it was.

"You could put on the brakes, Meg!" she said.

"Brakes!" That hadn't occurred to me. Brakes. My two modes are one hundred miles per hour or full stop. Moderation does not come easily to me.

"Go gently with the mower," my friend said.

"Gently!?" I thought. I'm not gentle with anything. I have been given lesson after lesson by the minions of physics—gravity, entropy, momentum, and inertia.

Is it possible to make friends with the physical world and with the way things are? Is it possible to feel affection for the stresses of machinery, the limitations of the body, the patterns of the way things happen? Would that affection help me move more fluidly through the rest of my life?

I'm intimately acquainted with the patterns of thought and emotion. Those are in my field of experience and expertise. I can tell you why people do most of what they do, what they are likely to do next, what will be too hard, what will twist a spirit, what will trigger the automatic shut-off in a heart.

I still push those well-known rules in my own relationships, though. I still make mistakes by being too rough, too honest at times, not honest enough at others. I'm learning. It's hard to learn how to be gentle when you like to push the pedal to the metal.

Maybe for today I will try a stance of gentle affection for the way things are, the way people are, and, oh yeah, for the way I am too. 'Cause sooner or later, I'll forget. Sooner or later, I'm going to floor it, baby.

A Different Garden

⤳

When I was about seven years old, my mother, sister, and I
lived with great-aunt Jean for a while across a small brown
pond from my grandparents' house. Next to Aunt Jean's
was an exotic neighbor family, the Grunwalds. He was a
designer for the North Carolina furniture factories. I think
he was German. She was a tall, slender woman with her
hair up in a French chignon. It could be that my missionary family, with our Oriental rugs, Indian brass, and carved
teak, were exotic to them too. The walls in the Grunwald's
house were glass and the floors were polished blonde wood.
They had sleek European furniture on geometric rugs. I
remember oranges and yellows, cheer and quiet.

Their daughter was named Lilith. Years later I learned that
in ancient tradition, Lilith was Adam's first wife, before Eve.
She was so wild and disobedient that she was banned from
Eden and replaced with the nicer, sweeter Eve. That the
Grunwalds would name their daughter after this wild force
of nature tells me I'm not wrong in remembering them as a
contrast to my church-going, Bible-reading family.

Mrs. Grunwald was elegant. When my nose itched, I would
poke a finger in and scratch. Mama told me to brush the
outside of my nose lightly when it itched inside. Mrs.
Grunwald did that, and wasn't she lovely? Mama wanted
to be tall and elegant instead of cute and perky, and Mrs.
Grunwald was her ideal.

Lilith and I used to go down to the pond in the backyard to fish. We each had a stick, a string, and a safety pin with a worm on it. Most of the time we didn't put on any worms. We knew nothing about flies or lures. We never did catch anything, but I looked into the brown water and felt happy fishing with my friend, talking about nothing much. I knew it wasn't religion. The world of my grandparents revolved around the church, the Bible, the Lord. Few sentences were spoken without reference to one of these. Lilith's family talked about food, politics, travel, their time living in India, where Lilith was born.

Neither of us was as wild and disobedient as Lilith's namesake. I was a good little girl. I tried hard to be, anyway. I know I thought about God a lot, and I worried that He was disappointed in me. I knew my teachers always were, because I couldn't follow instructions. It looked like rebellion, when really it was an inability to fathom why the rules were there. Why does it matter that I write my name on the upper righthand corner of the paper? Why can't I get out of my seat to see what that noise is in the hall? I broke the rules because I couldn't keep them in mind.

Eventually I felt expelled from that Eden, from the heartfelt and dedicated certainties of my family's religion. I wasn't expelled, really. I walked out of that garden. I took it all so seriously that the rules didn't make sense to me. They contradicted the stories of joy and grace, of knowing God in your heart, and because of that, knowing the right thing to do. I didn't know that many people just let the doctrines lay in layers as a restful backdrop to real life. I was trying to grab all the pieces and fit them together. I couldn't make it happen and I couldn't let it go, so I threw up my hands in despair and left.

I didn't become disobedient and disruptive. Until recently.

Now I'm a Lilith for sure. I run back and forth outside the wall of the garden of certainties, jumping up to see the remembered landscape, pointing and questioning.

"Do you know this thing is there? Does that one not bother you? If I can get this gate open, don't some of y'all want to come out here with me?"

Most people in the garden of certainty don't want to come out. Certainty is hard to give up.

I remain fascinated by friends who didn't grow up in the church at all, people who have a vague notion of who Abraham is but couldn't tell you who his children and grandchildren were. What did their family talk about? What did they push against? What gave them comfort? Where did their sense of the world come from, their sense of what had been and was yet to be?

I'm grateful to Lilith and her family for a brief and elegant glimpse of another way to be, a glimpse of a different garden.

Peter and the Beanstalk

Driving to the mall with my two boys, I listened to my thirteen-year-old tell about a friend of his who is a vegetarian.

"Mom, at her house they had salad for lunch." He was scandalized. "Even her dad ate salad. In fact, he made the salad." My boy eats salad too, nearly every night for supper. He is six feet two and plays football. The exotic idea of having salad as the main course shocked him. "At least she's not a vegan," he sighed.

"Or a stage four vegan," added his older brother. "They don't eat anything that casts a shadow."

There was silence while we all pondered this.

"Nothing that casts a shadow?" I asked. In my twenty years as a therapist, I have learned that sometimes I'm so flummoxed I don't even know what to ask. Repeating the last few words is all I can do.

"Yeah," he said, like the brilliant sixteen-year-old child he is. "Only stuff that grows underground. Like beans."

I stifled a giggle. "Beans don't grow under the ground," I said.

"Yes they do. Like peanuts," he said in a deep, authoritative man-voice.

My children have picked up a family trait that makes them say things with authority whether or not they are sure of their absolute correctness, on the assumption that sounding right is almost as good as being right.

"Honey. Trust me," I said, laughing by now. "I've grown beans before. They cast a shadow." Bubbles rose through my body. I was helplessly delighted with these children.

"Wrong, Mom. They're in the same family as peanuts. It's in the name. Pea. Nuts."

His little brother and I were both laughing so hard now that we had trouble catching our breath. I considered pulling the car over to the side of the road so we wouldn't wreck.

His younger brother leaned forward from the back seat, and said "Pea. Nuts? We're not even talking about peanuts. We're talking about beans, you know, like Peter and the beanstalk."

Someone screamed. I think it was me. Fortunately we were parked in the lot of the mall now.

"Oh my God, my children! Where did I go wrong?" I banged my head on the steering wheel. "Peter and the beanstalk?"

It's so much fun to be completely cracked up by my children. It makes up for those more difficult teenage things, like disobeying, disrespecting, disappointing, just to mention the things that start with "D."

They are so much themselves. The mix of their strengths and weaknesses is so blended, it doesn't even make sense to wish for the weaknesses to go away. That would change the recipe of who they are. I sure hope I can remember that next time one of the "D" words comes up. Driving, drinking, and dating. We are going to need all our humor and the strength of a—um—beanstalk.

Peggy in Port Arthur

∿

Part of a conversation I overheard has stuck with me.

"It always comes down to a waitress named Peggy who lives in Port Arthur."

I thought, "That's a song."

A tune came to mind, kind of a sea shanty. I sang it into my cell phone, which records tunes in its "voice memo" feature.

Maybe there is something about the ocean in the song. Port Arthur is on the coast, I think. All I know about Port Arthur is that Hurricane Rita swept through it, in a season where there were too many furious hurricanes and many preachers with straight faces saying that God was punishing the wicked. It looked to me like Mother Nature was targeting the oil industry, but that's not a rational thought either.

I wrote a few lines of the song about Peggy. "It always comes down to a waitress named Peggy, she works in Port Arthur, third shift at the diner. She loves her daddy, big earrings, and Jesus."

Then I ground to a halt. I wasn't that curious about Peggy. What is "it all" anyway? The universe? Maybe that's too big; maybe the person meant a smaller "it." Maybe they were talking about a relationship. Maybe one of the part-

n love with Peggy long ago but wasn't able to be
        Now everything in the couple's relationship filters
through the original and ideal love for Peggy. Maybe this
person only met Peggy one time, or maybe they knew her
in high school. That love—that ideal which has outshone
everything since then—is just a dream, not real at all.
It's hard for a real love to compete with a dream of love.
Maybe that's what the song is about.

Maybe the singer was in the diner in the wee hours of the
morning, talking to Peggy in that way people do during
those hours outside of normal waking time, when two
strangers talk in low voices about things that are dark and
deep, things neither would speak of with the sun in the sky.

I decided to ask my friends what they thought about Peggy.
We say "Seminar question!" and that means we are invited
to think together for fun.

"Okay," I asked, "Say it always comes down to a waitress
named Peggy who lives in Port Arthur. What is 'it'?"

"The meaning of life," one friend says. "I think the waitress
said something to the person that stuck with them. You
know how sometimes when you hear something, it just
jumps out of its context, blows up to three times its size and
vibrates, changing colors, and becomes about everything?"

"Yes, I do," I said. "That's what Peggy has done in my
mind, but I can't figure out how she is about everything."

Another said, "It's that you know her name. The connection between you is important. When you ask her how she is, do you really care? When she asks you how you are, does she really care? Do you tell her? Are you treating her right? Don't you know who that lady is? She's Jesus Christ. You remember in the last paragraph of Salinger's *Franny and Zooey*, Seymour says that the fat lady on the sofa listening to the radio is Jesus Christ. He says 'Dammit, don't you understand? They're all Jesus Christ.'"

Someone else said, "I think Peggy knows why this world is so mucked up."

The last person I asked said, "It all comes down to just getting by—putting one foot in front of the other. It's people like that who make things go."

This must be another projective test, like the inkblots therapists use. What you see reveals more about you than about the inkblot. I don't know much more about Peggy, but I learned what was in the minds of my friends.

They say people who have near-death experiences hear two questions as they approach the light: How did you serve other people? Did you figure out the way things work?

Peggy knows how to answer both questions, I think. Maybe she is a bodhisattva, one of those enlightened ones who choose to stay on the earth as teachers for the rest of us.

They are everywhere. What are they telling us? If I said it out loud it would sound too simple. Listen to Peggy as she whispers in your ear.

What do you hear from the mouth of the enlightened one as she brings you your coffee?

Laughing It Off?

In a workshop on multiculturalism, some black participants were talking ruefully about how each of them has at least one "doppelganger," someone with whom the white folks consistently confuse them. Apparently brown skin is such an identifier for white people that some will confuse a small woman with walnut-colored skin and a two-inch afro with a much larger caramel-complexioned woman with long dreadlocks, simply because they are both black.

I understand how that happens. I tend to mix up slender blonde white women unless I know them well. And I'm white. And blonde. I know that getting one black woman mixed up with another can be racist, simply because the observer, for some reason, hasn't trained herself or himself to look deeper into a black person's face to see if there are freckles, frown lines, an impish set to the lips, upturned eyes, or a serious expression.

I spoke out and said this in the workshop, and then added that some of the straight folks in my congregation get the lesbian couples mixed up with one another. In a couple made up of two middle-aged women with short salt-and-pepper hair and sensible shoes, people ask, "Are you Cindy or the other one?"

I laughed as I told that, because it's funny to me. It needs to be changed, but it's still funny.

"This is not something to laugh off," said an elder activist sternly from the podium. He had a full head of white hair and jet black eyebrows that made his face striking. He seemed very serious, determined that this concern would not be diluted with humor.

I found myself wanting to shoot back, "Just because I laugh doesn't mean I'm laughing it off."

He did get me thinking. The women who were ahead of me in seminary worried that if we laughed we wouldn't be taken seriously. Activists of all kinds are notoriously grim. I might be wrong to laugh. Maybe laughing is a luxury. Maybe you can't afford it until there is enough safety, enough justice.

One thing I don't understand is the either/or thinking. Why is it that you either laugh or do something to change things? Can't we do both? Why can't we laugh at the stupidity of white folks seeing only brown skin instead of seeing a whole person, and work like hell to deepen the ways we see one another? Why can't we laugh at some straight folks seeing only "lesbian" instead of "outgoing," "quiet," or "humorous"? At some young people only seeing "elderly." At some men only seeing "fat woman." At some women seeing only "suit."

Maybe I'm wrong. Maybe seeing the laughable bits of the way we are enables us to live with them rather than becoming determined to change them. I'm becoming willing to be convinced that this is the danger, but I'm not convinced yet.

We need to deepen our identifiers of people, to see them as brown-skinned and shy, or blonde and athletic, or lesbian and green-eyed. That's a skill, a stance of generous curiosity about other folks that soulful people might want to develop. You can laugh about something as a way of pointing out that it's not the way you want it to be. After all, most of the early peer training children give one another in how to be, how to look, how to behave, is done through laughter. It's not nice laughter, but it does enforce a rigid code quite successfully.

Could we jeer one another into behaving more intelligently? Would we want to? I don't really think so; I don't like mean laughter, but I'm noticing that stern and humorless exhortation is not working, and our inability to really see one another has big economic, social, and spiritual consequences.

I see life as funny pretty often. I don't believe in laughing at someone's expense, like when they fall down or make a mistake. I stopped male-bashing when my first son was born.

If someone tells an ethnic joke, I tell them my daddy was from whatever group it is they are joking about. Once, a drunken man at a party told me a joke about black people. I balled my hands into fists and told him my daddy was black. He was horrified, not at being a racist, which is acceptable in far too many circles, but at having the bad manners to guess wrongly about my affiliations. My daddy wasn't black, but he could have been. I'm hoping that man will never be as confident again that you can tell by looking.

Anyway, jokes are a tiny portion of what's funny in this world. What is funny is how ridiculous we are, how righteous we pretend to be, how often we get caught with our pretensions hanging out. My thought is that the more you refuse to laugh, the more you attract the attention of the Karma Fairy, the one who makes certain that some day soon you will be caught in the very same behavior you decry with your fiery righteousness.

I'm going to keep laughing, and I will do my best to include being amused by my own behavior. And I will try to see the humor the next time someone gets me mixed up again with some other large-ish white woman who looks nothing like me. Then I will make sure they remember what I look like next time.

Singing the Soup

An ice storm hit this part of the South the other night, and our house is still without power. The world looks spectacular covered in ice, like all the trees are made of Waterford crystal, catching the light and scattering it in a confetti of rainbows. The beauty makes me catch my breath. It almost makes up for the fact that I can't get warm and now I'm worrying three times as much about all those people in my town I worry about all the time anyway.

Some magic happened last night. Nancy, a church member who is famous for her soup and her bread, called to say she had vegetables in her fridge that weren't long for this world. She offered to come to the church, where there was power, to make soup for people without power. We converged on the church and I gave her my own big bag of vegetables that had seen better days. She sorted through them all, discarding bits that were already gone over to the slimy side. She chopped what was left, taking care to leave out the peppers, as one of the expected guests was allergic. The sugar peas glowed like jewels on her cutting board. She moved calmly, not cussing at all, unlike me when I'm cooking. She knew which vegetables to put into the soup first, which ones needed extra sautéing so they would be soft enough, and which had to wait until right near the end to go in, so they would hold up.

My first singing teacher used to tell me all the notes should come out at about the same level of intensity and volume, and it looked to me like Nancy was doing that with the vegetables. She was singing that soup.

I went into the office to work and be warm. Nancy had also brought three loaves of wheat bread ready to rise and a couple of loaves of cinnamon raisin. Every time I emerged from the office, the building smelled better and better. The bread came out of the oven a little before folks were supposed to get there, and she offered me the heel of one of the cinnamon-raisin loaves hot, with fresh butter.

Church members with no power began to arrive. The ones with small children looked the most stressed. The little ones didn't understand why they couldn't watch videos or have their milk warmed up. Reports came in of folks with power giving shelter to those without power. People were checking on one another the best they could with so many phones not working and hardly any cell phone service.

We decided the cold wasn't as bad as the darkness, that we missed showers less than we missed reading. We traded techniques for reading by flashlight. Others with power had brought food too, so we had plenty. We decided that, since we seem to get one of these ice storms every three years or so, we would just make it common knowledge that, on the first full day without power, we would have a soup supper at the church.

It is warm to gather with members of your community and endure a hardship together. It is nourishing to see people forming the desire to care for one another and then acting on it. This kind of behavior from church members can sustain a minister's heart. This whole community is like a good soup, with ingredients brought by everyone, lots of colors, flavors, and textures that can feed a body and a soul.

It makes my soul sing.

Silence

The wise man in the teaching story said he had decided never again to utter an unnecessary word. He was silent for the next twelve years. The story didn't say what persuaded the wise man to break his silence. That would have been important information. The story makes me mad.

I do understand the beauty and the power of silence. In conversations with clients, with my children, with parishioners, I stay silent sometimes as a way to give them space to figure things out on their own, and oftentimes they do. In my office I have a carved wooden mask of a woman's face, and she is holding one finger up to her lips. She reminds me to say less. Sometimes that works. Why does the teaching story make me so mad? I guess because it teaches not to say unnecessary words. But I wonder what makes a word necessary.

I have done couples counseling for nearly twenty years now, and silence does as much damage to a relationship as hard words. Sweet words strengthen the bond between people. We need to hear that we are loved, that we look good, that we did a great job, that we are appreciated. Those are necessary words. I have known people who have starved to death emotionally in relationships where their partners didn't believe in saying unnecessary words. Some folks think that talking is only good for exchanging information or giving advice. You say, "Talk to me about your day," and they say, "It's nothing you haven't heard before. No new information." You say, "Tell me how you feel." and they answer, "It wouldn't do any good. It wouldn't fix the situation."

Stories that families tell carry history and identity. Stories friends tell to one another, about one another, create bonds and memories that can support a life when it's sagging. I talked with my sister on the phone last night. Our beloved friend Pat and his seven-year-old son spent a day with them last month in Texas. Now, Pat's a talker, and so is his boy, and so is my brother-in-law. My sister's children are now telling Pat stories, imitating his voice as they remember lines from his stories. One day at a party Pat was telling a woman that he was jealous of a friend: "Charles is better looking than me, richer than me, he's more successful than me and he's funnier than me." The woman said, "Oh, Pat, he's not funnier than you." Last night on the phone my sister gave the receiver to her eight-year-old daughter so she could deliver the punch line to me. Her little girl voice said, in a dead-on Forest City, North Carolina accent, "Oh Pat, he's not funnier than you!"

I want to say to that silent wise man, "Mr. Wise Man, I hope you are not in a relationship and I hope you don't have any children, and I hope you don't have any friends. If you do, shame on you for not thinking it necessary to say every day, 'I love you,' or 'How are you?' or 'Tell me your day.' I hope you live in a hermitage far away from folks who need you or love you. Maybe you live with one very understanding cat—and I hope you pat her."

A Pirate Is a Rabbi

I was listening to the radio in the car one day and I thought I heard Bob Marley sing something like "A pirate is a rabbi." That's all I heard. What a poetic line!

It got me thinking about the people who have told me about the time when they lost everything and how much that time taught them. A pirate takes everything you've got and a rabbi is a teacher. Maybe that's what Bob Marley meant: The one who steals your riches also teaches you what's important in life. You are not your wealth or your position. Your infinite worth is inside of you.

Facing the loss of everything makes you ask yourself questions. What's wrong with me? How did I get myself in this situation? Why didn't I save instead of spend? Why didn't I appreciate what I had when I had it? If I could have it back, I would drop to my knees and kiss the floor of that house I loved, that garden I grumbled about. I would take those healthy legs for a walk every night, and now I can't. I was beautiful; I had so much. Why didn't I notice?

You wonder if it's time to pray now that you are facing such loss. You worry that you didn't pray much when things were good. You wonder if the universe will keep taking care of you the way it did before. Why should it? After all, it doesn't take care of everyone. You can see that just by looking around. You have been one of the lucky ones.

A pirate can capture you and take you on a journey against your will, far from what is familiar. Your identity can be stripped away as you leave life as you know it behind. You may discover what you can survive. You will learn things about yourself and about the world that many people don't have to learn. These are things the rabbis try to make you think about, but you don't have the time, the inclination, or the interest. When you lose everything, suddenly your interest in these matters intensifies.

There is a freedom, I hear, in knowing that you've survived the loss of everything. You know you will eventually get through to the other side. You've come through the fire. Everything in you that was straw and plywood is burned away. But those things, those qualities, that are sure and deep, that shine like rubies, that endure like rock—those are still there. You are now made of stronger stuff. You don't have to live in fear.

My attention returned to Bob Marley's song, but I couldn't make out all the words. Something about freeing your mind from mental slavery, singing redemption songs.

When I got home, I looked online for the lyrics. Bob was singing, "Old pirates yes they rob I."

I couldn't understand the words, but I got the gist.

Thanks, Bob.

Samaritan

Like most of America, I have been watching images of war and natural disasters on my television. I try to imagine New Orleans right after Katrina hit: The music has fallen silent, the kitchens are still and sour instead of bustling and fragrant. People on the streets look stunned. I try to imagine spending two days with my tall teenage sons in a shelter where we have no water, no food. We hear babies crying with hunger and see drunks without their drink, addicts without their fix, mentally unstable people without their medicine, and everyone reaching their breaking point, reverting to their stress behaviors. The veneer of civilization is cracking. No one knows when it will end. We're all aching to know when help will come and why it hasn't arrived already.

Sometimes I try to imagine my family as really poor, trying to live on minimum wage. Every day is a crisis. I think I would give up after a week of the kind of life that some people wake up to every morning. I can't stretch my life experience far enough to subtract not only my car but my in-home washer and dryer, my bug-free house, my good foundation of health and dental care, my trust-inspiring, white female face. What would life be without these? I meet people at church, in my town, who know the answer. I watch as they reach out to the government, to me, and I struggle to open my heart to all that suffering, to look it full in the face and grieve with them and yet keep going forward with my life.

I think of the parable of the Good Samaritan, a story I was raised on. The good man on the road passes a stranger who has been beaten and robbed and left in a ditch. He helps him, gets him a place to stay and food and clothes. That's how I'm supposed to be. But what if there was a stranger in the ditch every time the Samaritan walked that road? What if there were ten? A hundred? Every time? What would he do then? The need is overwhelming.

I don't know what to do. I don't know how to think about this. It's all I can do not to look away. Sometimes I write a check. Sometimes when I shop for toiletries, I add extra into the cart for donations. The people in my church help all the time, gathering food and daily essentials for the school near us.

It's one step at a time, one thing after another, deciding every day whether to look and help or look away. I don't blame people for wanting to rest, to look away for a time. You can only be on the front lines for a short while, then you have to drop back and let others take your place. I feel strong right now, but who knows how long it will last? I do what I can.

There are so many heroes in a time of disaster. But there are also people who help by doing small things often, even in ordinary times. I think of the words of Adrienne Rich in the back of my church's hymnbook:

My heart is moved by all I cannot save:
So much has been destroyed
I have to cast my lot with those who, age after age,
Perversely, with no extraordinary power, reconstitute
the world.

Revlon, Max Factor, Neutrogena, Maybelline

The signs on the shelves in the pharmacy section of the store listed: Revlon, Max Factor, Neutrogena, Maybelline. I rolled my cart past the aisle and the rhythm of a new song started in my head.

"Revlon, Max Factor, Neutrogena, Maybelline……. Cover Girl, Almay, make me look like a magazine. Revlon, Max Factor, Neutrogena, Maybelline, Cover Girl, Almay, make me into a beauty queen."

I have tried to learn about makeup at various times in my life. Some internal signal will sound and I will think, "I need to fluff up a bit." I've read about shading under my cheekbones and down the sides of my nose, about what would bring out the color of my eyes, about warm colors and cool colors. I wore thick mascara as a teenager over my dad's objections. He liked the way I looked without it better. When I got to college I stopped. It turned out he was right.

"Revlon, Max Factor, Neutrogena, Maybelline……. Cover Girl, Almay, make me look like a magazine."

As the chant repeated in my head, I thought about the beauties I know. It's not their skin. It's how fierce they are, or how kind. It's the way they laugh, rich and spicy.

One of them shimmered with beauty when she stamped her foot and said, "I don't care if I offend my family with my politics. They have shared theirs with me over the years, and I have been silent. I'm not going to be silent any more."

One of my friends is beautiful because of the way she carries herself. She does yoga and rides horses, and she walks proud and strong. She does wear some makeup, but I don't think it changes the way she walks.

It is fun to wear makeup sometimes, to decorate my face. I like wearing lipstick, which is quick, and eyeliner, when I have patience, or when there is a stoplight that gives me time to put it on in the car. It can brighten up my face or give some color, but I would argue that it doesn't make us beautiful.

I have met so many of you who read or listen to my stories on the radio. You speak to me after book signings, speeches across the country, and church meetings. In a way I carry you with me. I hold you in my mind and heart and I feel you living your lives there where you are, as I live mine here. I envision how beautiful you are when you speak respectfully to those with whom you disagree, even though you are passionate about the disagreement. I see how beautiful you are when you hand me something you've read or written that you think I will enjoy; you hand it to me with a mixture of nonchalance and eagerness. I see how you shine when you ask questions about faith and doubt, when you tell a story from your childhood, when you let me see your temper or your sorrow.

For so much of my life I have felt plain. My father, who nicknamed me "gorgeous," also made side comments about how this one part of me was lovely, or that part. Like he was trying to find something to be positive about.

I know how that started. I had crossed eyes when I was born. Several operations later, there is still a little drift. I was almost always too heavy for current standards, and weight was a big thing in my father's family when he was growing up. Also, he had been the plainest sibling among four, the three others angelically beautiful. So he told me I was smart, and that a brain was more important than prettiness.

I look at pictures of myself from my teen years. The funny thing? I was gorgeous. How did I not know I was so beautiful? How did my sister and I think we had "thunder thighs"? How did my friends and I think we were too dark, too white, too fat, too short, too busty? We walked in beauty. It was before us and behind us, above us and all around us, and it still is.

Can we know right now that we are beautiful? Can we know that, when we are old, we will look at pictures of us now and say, "How could I not know that I was beautiful?" Can we know that it's our smile, the way we carry ourselves, what we find to think about, how we talk about what we read, how we handle our anger, how we admit when we're wrong? It's our honesty and our humor, our history and our kindness.

They shouldn't call it the beauty aisle, that place in the store with all the makeup. Call it the decoration aisle. I know what beauty is. It's not in the store. It's everywhere. May it be above you, below you, and all around you.

River

~:

A few years ago I was at the end of a chapter in my life. An interim ministry job I loved was finished, and I didn't know what I would do next. When I'm flummoxed, a trip to the thrift store is in order. Usually I buy a shirt, a jacket, or some glasses for the kitchen.

But these were unusual circumstances. My heart was breaking. I missed my church people. I was scared and I didn't know where the money would come from to support my children. A shirt would not do in this situation.

What I bought was a massive maple console turntable. My sons and I wrestled the enormous thing into the house. Under its lid was an automatic changer, a radio, and an eight-track tape deck. We trooped down to the basement and dug out my LPs, which I hadn't played since college. I put on Joni Mitchell's Blue.

Listening as the music filled the house, I was overcome with an image of the young woman I used to be standing next to the woman I am now. The words to "River" wove around and through me:

"I'm so hard to handle," Joni sang. "I'm selfish and I'm sad…."

I thought about the nineteen-year-old I was when I last put a needle on that record. Back then, I didn't know I was hard to handle too. There was a lot I didn't know. Because of that, I think there was much I couldn't feel.

When I was in college, the only other living thing I had to take care of was a plant, and it struggled for its life. I knew I wanted to be a therapist, but back then I thought that was about giving good advice. I thought I was fat then; what would I give now to have that body again. I wouldn't want that naiveté back. I wouldn't want that anger and confusion. I wouldn't want that hopefulness, the arrogant health, the judgmental certainty of right and wrong. I wouldn't want to be at the beginning of my journey instead of where I am now.

Joni sang, "I wish I had a river I could skate away on."

I never felt as sad when I listened to the song at nineteen as I do now. I didn't know then what she meant, how she felt, why one would want to skate away. Since then I have skated away from my first marriage. I skated away from my childhood religion. Both escapes brought grief and relief, fear and freedom. Skating faster, more surefooted as I went, I found my balance and my rhythm. Around this current bend in the river, life was good. This life made sense to me.

I am the mother of two boys now. Their father and I were married for seventeen years. It was a good marriage. Just because it ended doesn't mean it was never any good, that the love between us wasn't real. Our two boys are a gift to the world. They are funny, smart, and handsome, and they are starting to like some of the music I listened to back then.

It was too much to hope that they would enjoy Joni Mitchell, but the other day one of them said he'd heard a song by Led Zeppelin that was cool. We downloaded the song and when we pushed "play" I had that sense again of my younger self standing next to me.

Robert Plant's voice used to fill my virginal bedroom at night when I was fifteen. His voice held most of what I knew about sex back then. We listened to it pouring out of the speakers of our iMac, my teenage sons standing behind me, for some reason all of us looking at the computer screen. I skated away from my parents on those songs. Hurtling across the ice of my own river back then, falling, picking myself up, setting out again to see what was around the next curve.

When the river doubles back on itself and I get to see, for an instant, where and who I used to be. Music is one of the elements that can waft across time, reach around the next bend and give a little glimpse of both selves at once. I can almost wave to myself as I fly past.

I saw my fifteen-year-old bent over my guitar yesterday playing "Blackbird." He looked so much like his father at the beginning of our marriage, bent over his guitar playing "Blackbird." My older son has learned it too. That made me smile. I hope one day they will teach it to their children. I hope their skate will be a joyous one, and that music will give them a glimpse of who they are next to who they used to be. I hope they are glad of what they see.

Straight Through the Heart

ᴗ:

My older son might as well have taken a knife and stabbed me in the heart. I know teens experiment. I know they try on different ways of being until they find the one that will drive you the most crazy. I know it doesn't mean they are bad people if they are different from me. But this?

"Mom, I think I might want to take accounting classes in school," he said.

Accounting classes? How could he be this different from me? I get tax forms in the mail and I break into a sweat holding them gingerly by the corner, carrying them to the patient woman who does my taxes.

I have always known this boy was an orderly person. When he was just learning to roll over, maybe five months old, I left him on the living room floor while I went into the kitchen to make a grilled cheese sandwich. A night-light in the shape of a seashell had fallen out of its outlet above the floor molding. It had been lying on its back on the floor for a day or two, waiting for me to get the wave of energy to bend over and put it back into the outlet. When I returned to the living room with my sandwich, my son had rolled the twelve feet over to the wall and was trying to put the light back into its outlet. At that moment, I caught a glimpse of the person he would become.

Orderly is good. I see the need for that quality in the world. I wish I had more of it. It's a strange feeling, though, to see a quality in my child that doesn't appear in either me or his father, a quality that just shows up like a stranger at a family reunion.

When the boys were babies, my friends and I would speculate on what our children could do to drive us crazy. Could the boys wear mascara? Get their noses pierced? Shave half their heads and dye the rest green?

Several months ago I was joking with him that he would find a way to drive me crazy pretty soon.

"I know exactly how I could do it," my son said. "Become a Baptist Republican."

Oh God. He hit it on the nose. That is what is going to happen. Okay. I can live with that. Will I take a deep breath and applaud his columns in the National Review? Can I help him drive his Sunday school class to the Promise Keepers rally? Can I love his extremely sweet wife in her white socks and white Keds and the bow in her hair as big as a pie plate?

We'll see when the time comes. I will breathe deeply and get used to it. He will be different from me. It will be okay. Maybe he can do my taxes.

That's the Job

~:~

The ring tone on my cell phone plays the theme from the TV show *Rockford Files*. I used to watch that show in the afternoons after school. Jim Rockford was tough, but when the bad guys beat him up he had bruises for days. Sometimes his back went out. His car was cool and powerful, a Pontiac Firebird Esprit, but it broke down sometimes. He was easygoing, but it was a struggle for him to be patient with his dad and with his friend Angel. When he was angry he would yell. His friends were loyal, but they tended to take advantage of him. No one on that show was all good, all powerful; no one made the right decision all the time. Rockford was a hero with wide streaks of humanity.

I work as a minister these days, and it's a funny kind of job. I have to watch out or people will treat me like a hero. I could start to think I have lots of answers, that I can make things happen, or that I should be nice instead of being good. There's a big difference. The job itself is impossible, because people's hearts need more ministering than one person can do, not to mention their minds and their bodies. That's not even touching the need to research and write a sermon a week. Or the meetings. All I can do is the next thing that needs doing. Sometimes it's the thing right in front of me, but sometimes the urgent-looking thing in front of me is just a distraction from what is really important.

I like to think of being a Jim Rockford kind of minister,

taking things on without too much fanfare, knowing I will have bruises and fall down on a regular basis, fairly confident that if I keep at it, I can do a pretty good job.

My mentor, Jim Rockford, wasn't sure of the outcome of a case when he took it. He never bragged to a client that he was the best. He didn't like to take out his gun. Mostly he just kept at things. He pulled at loose ends until they led him somewhere. He just did his job, whether it took him to the homes of the rich and powerful or to a trailer park at the end of nowhere. The rich didn't intimidate him, and the powerful only slowed him down some. He didn't trust people naively, because people will do what they are going to do, and they don't always want you to know about it. Twenty years as a therapist have taught me the same thing.

Now, whenever my phone rings, whether it's someone who has just had a bad diagnosis, someone who has an idea for something the church should do, or someone who wants to come talk, I'm reminded of my mentor. If someone comes to me for counseling and they say, "No one else has been able to help me with this," I can answer, "Then I probably won't be able to help you either, but I sure will give it a shot."

I can calm down my inner-perfectionist, first-born, Virgo, overachieving self by holding Rockford in my mind. I slide into the seat of the Firebird, crank the ignition, and go off to get the job done. By the end I may have a few bruises, I may have lost my temper once or twice, and my back might go out.

But hey, that's the job.

Seagal Therapy

One of my seldom-confessed weaknesses is an irrational fondness for bad Steven Seagal movies. I know that's an oxy**mo**ron, but there you go. I just saw the movie *On Deadly Ground*, and it was a real eye-opener for me.

For one thing, I realized that we therapists have been going about things all wrong. Steven Seagal changed a man's whole personality in a bar fight; it took maybe ten minutes. The man was a walking, talking stereotype, a big old oil-derrick worker tormenting a poor Native man. Excuse me, a poor drunk Native American man. In this movie there was no one who escaped stereotyping. The big ol' roughneck was humiliating the poor drunk man, pushing him around.

Here's what Seagal did about it. I'll describe his technique simply, using no therapeutic jargon whatsoever.

He punched the man three times in the stomach 'til the guy threw up. In a minute, the man staggered to his feet.

Steven Seagal said quietly, "How do you change the essence of a man?"

The roughneck, blood flowing from his nose, said, I swear to God, "I need time . . . to change."

It was a great comic moment. Or was it a cosmic moment? Sometimes the two are hard to tell apart.

It was transformation the easy way. Maybe Seagal will establish the "punch people in the stomach till they throw up" school of therapy. Maybe new churches will spring up, trying out the "punch them in the stomach" way to repentance.

Transformation in real life takes longer than that for most of us. Everybody wants it to be faster than it is. I have had people come into my office for counseling who have never been happy, never felt good about their lives, and never had a deep relationship. They want me to fix them up, and they want to know exactly how long it's going to take.

I understand. I want fast transformation too. I would love it if there were twenty easy steps a person could do to become whole and joyful, hopeful and healthy. I would love it if the twenty steps could be done just once and—presto—it's all fixed! And maybe the whole process could take about six weeks. I would also be grateful if the process of zipping to wholeness would involve no punching and no throwing up.

It would be great if someone opened a Soul Spa, where you could check in and have your emotional baggage unpacked in your room while you were in the hot tub. You could put your messed up thoughts and feelings out in the hall. While you slept, they would be spirited away and returned in the morning, cleaned, pressed, and mended. A psyche massage would release all the accumulated toxins while you relaxed.

Maybe someone will come up with that. Meanwhile, transformation is usually painful. But not as bad as Steven

93

Seagal punching you three times in the stomach in front of your friends. You know what? I would try it myself if I thought it would change my eating and exercise habits. Three punches would be nothing compared to what I've already tried.

Honestly though? I don't believe in Seagal Therapy, so I think I'll stick with the methods I've been using, both for doing therapy and trying to change myself—and I will continue to relax, guiltily, in front of Seagal's magnificently awful movies.

Sparklers on the Deck

My Uncle Toby only ever visited us once. Out of the blue, one afternoon, he called. No one was home but me. I answered the phone and an old-man voice said, "Hey, little girl, this is your Uncle Toby. I've been poisoning pigeons in the park, and I want to come see you."

Uncle Toby came to supper that night. My mother, surprised with company from California after teaching second-graders all day, was sweet and darling. Cooking hamburgers, participating in the conversation, she moved from the deck to the kitchen and back out again. Uncle Toby said to her, "Kathy, you look more like a school teacher every time I see you. She bristled at that. It hadn't sounded like a compliment. He was amazed that her feelings were hurt. I don't know whether he was pretending, whether it was meanness or misunderstanding.

I didn't know the man, but I learned a little when he started telling stories.

On their honeymoon, Toby and his wife Gertrude went to Niagara Falls. They borrowed a camera from a neighbor. While in a cable car, suspended over the falls, Gertrude dropped the camera out of her lap right as they were about to come into the platform. Toby saw the camera snagged on a rock halfway down the cliff.

Back at the hotel, he said "Gertrude, I'm going for the camera. I'll be back." He left to climb hand over hand down the cliff into the mist.

After three hours, she began to worry. After five hours, the hotel manager gave her his sympathies and said she should not expect her husband back. Just then Toby appeared, filthy, his shirt torn, with the camera in his hand. He had held it in his teeth, he said, all the way back up the cliff.

It wouldn't have been such a big deal, he explained to us, but the camera was borrowed. He didn't want his beloved to feel bad about losing it. He had only recently been able to fall in love again, he said, after losing his first love. It had taken him seven years to get over her. All the cells in your body are new after seven years, Uncle Toby explained. That woman had been in every cell of his body.

It was good to hear about a love like that. And a new love found. It was good to hear about bravery and derring-do.

It was fully dark by then. Mama pulled out some sparklers and did a cheerleader routine using the sparklers as pom-poms. My sister and I wrote our names with light in the black air. We threw our heads back and laughed.

No one had a camera that night, but my memory took a picture of loving, of hurt, of kindness, shared food, night air, storytelling, dancing, and fireworks.

Family. It's been more than seven years, but they are still in every cell.

Whinny

I don't remember when I started going crazy for horses. I remember drawing a horse's head when I was in second grade. Well, I traced it, but I told my mother I drew it. I heard the surprise in her voice as she exclaimed over how good it was. I lived with the guilt after that for about three hours, then I tearfully told her the truth. She was nice about it; she hugged me and said I did the right thing by confessing.

I remember the night I went to the mall with six dollars in my hands. I spread the money like a fan, walking fast to the store where they sold plastic model horses. It was more money than I had ever held before. I might have been eleven. Maybe twelve, because I was on my own at the mall. I remember the velvet feeling of the night air, the fizz of excitement in my chest about getting a new horse, a new friend. This one was a big butterscotch horse rearing up and looking stern and full of wisdom.

The high windowsills of my 1960s bedroom were lined with model horses. In fifth grade I would feed them all at night, holding a handful of imaginary hay up to each plastic mouth, my heart aching with love and anxiety. Would I leave any one out? Would their feelings be hurt? Would I take care of them adequately? That got to be too much trouble and fretting, so I told myself they didn't really have to eat and forgot about feeding them.

Some people say this thing between girls and horses is about sex; some say it's about power. I think it's about beauty and God. I know all four of these are related. My plastic horses were icons. Although they were made with human hands, they carried a bit of the horses' divinity in them, their beauty, nobility, strength, and speed. Does Divinity actually come to reside in an icon? Or were the plastic models just tangible containers for what I worshipped in my heart? Were they screens onto which I could project my inner strength and speed, my inner nobility and beauty? When my family had some money I took riding lessons, I had a black velvet-covered helmet and shiny boots. I learned to jump small fences, how to get the horse to lead with first one leg and then the other as we broke into a canter. I liked the smell of the horse, the thud of his hoofs on the packed dirt, the sudden silence flying over the jump, the grunt and impact of landing.

The summer I was fourteen, we did not have money. I rode at a run-down stable, kept going (barely) by a grizzled man named Howard. My friend Lois and I taught each other. We dreamed of show jumping. Howard didn't take good care of the place; he smelled like a drunk; and once in a while he found something on the front of our T-shirts that needed to be brushed off. It was uncomfortable. I didn't know what to think about it.

One afternoon, jumping a horse over the fences inside the ring, I was thrown off. The horse wanted to be back at the barn, and he jumped the fence that circled the ring, landing at a full gallop. I hit my head on a rock, had amnesia for a few days, and never rode again.

Sex, power, beauty, and God collided at Howard's place and made a mess.

I limp now from that fall, from wrestling—like ancient Jacob with his hip put out of joint from wrestling an angel, demanding that it bless him.

I have wrestled mightily in my life with the angels of sex, power, beauty, and God. I've been generously blessed and just a little broken.

It's been quite a ride.

Watery Wedding

❧

We were afraid it might rain on the wedding. The bride and groom were both paddlers who had met on the water, both over fifty, divorced long ago from other people. Their wedding was on top of Parris Mountain at a lodge by the lake.

The couple had planned to have the ceremony out by the water. An archway with vines wound through it framed a view of the lake. The day before, we rehearsed the ceremony both inside and outside so that we could keep our options open.

The wedding day was cloudy. It rained on and off. I arrived for the ceremony and the groom met me in the driveway to tell me that the TV Doppler radar had given us an hour-and–a-half window of relatively dry air to work with.

The piano player set up his keyboard outside. He and I laughed together. I told him the couple had decided on new music and did he know "Yummy Yummy Yummy, I've Got Love in My Tummy." All the chairs were set up outside and decorated with tulle. It was time to start. The clouds hung heavy as the wedding began. The mothers of the couple walked down the hill to their chairs to the tune of "Embraceable You." The bride and groom walked toward one another from opposite ends of the yard to meet at the archway. The music for their coming together was "Taking a Chance on Love."

Taking a chance on love. Taking a chance on rain. In my tradition, one line of the vows says, "loving what I know of you, trusting what I do not yet know." Two people declaring in front of family and friends that they have faith in one another and in the future. They have faith in one another to cook and make love and paddle and read and talk and look out the window together. To build a life together.

For a long time, I was dead set against marrying again. One divorce was enough for me. It was a good marriage for as long as it lasted. I don't think of it as a mistake. My sons are tangible evidence that it was not. I loved their father like crazy back then. If I loved that much and it didn't last, what was the point of trying again?

During that wedding a dammed-up place broke open inside me. Suddenly marriage seemed possible again. The bride and groom looked like the king and queen of the water sprites. Her dress was black and royal blue, shimmering and changing as she moved. We spoke the words that made the ceremony move and turn. Water had been so central in their relationship that the couple decided to incorporate it into their wedding. I poured water into two goblets, and they drank from their own and then each other's goblets. In the course of their lives together, they had been on still water and on white water. Passion, like water, can heal and cleanse or it can destroy. We spoke of respecting the power of both forces.

Halfway through the ceremony, the rain started, slowly and gently. I murmured to the couple that, until the rain got heavy, I was going to keep going. As we spoke about water, tiny droplets freckled our clothes. It was perfect—better than if the rain had held off. The ritual was surrounded by the element of water—of flow, of emotion, of the humility of seeking the lowest level, of persisting. Water, the softest thing on earth that nourishes everything that lives and can carve solid rock. The soul is the only thing richer. Love is the only thing stronger.

Soul, love, water—we were drenched in all of these on the mountain that day.

Life Without Meryl

Well, it looks like I'll never hang out with Meryl Streep in Manhattan. I met an actress one time who came down here to give a talk at the college where I was teaching. She and I hit it off, and she said, "Meryl would love you! Next time you come to New York, call me and we'll all have lunch." Then I had a baby, then another, and I didn't get to New York again until my sons were teenagers.

Last night, for the first time, I remembered the actress's offer, and I regretted that I never followed through. Maybe Meryl and I would have hit it off. Maybe we would have laughed together over the years about raising kids, the excesses of certain directors, what it was like to get out on white water, how long we like to stay in the bathtub.

Maybe I'm at some kind of transition point in life; all the things I have not yet done are very much with me. They all seemed like possibilities once. If I just steered a little more this way or that, I could end up almost anywhere. Now it feels as if most of my choices have been made. I like the way things are, don't get me wrong. I love my house, the people in my household, my work, the patterns and rhythms of the days. My children are wonderful people. I'm stunned with the blessing of having them in my life.

But I've realized that I won't ever be able, now, to do enough of a beauty routine to be young and stunning.

The thought makes me smile. I probably won't be an outlaw hero, like Harriet Tubman, bravely flouting the law in order to bring justice and right into the world, my name remembered for stubborn courage and persistence. I did have a great-, great-, great grandfather who became an outlaw in Ireland for teaching Gaelic to the children, under penalty of death. He was in his seventies when he began, in his nineties when he died. Maybe I will find something righteous to get in trouble for in my seventies.

I don't think that I will be a horse whisperer, taming and teaching them, showing them who they are in relation to the world in a different way. I'm not going to be a CIA agent, monitoring who is buying yellow-cake uranium in Africa, smoothly operating a double life, one person on the outside, quite another one in earnest, and perhaps someone else deep inside. I'm not going to be a test pilot for new air-craft. My eyes are not good any more. Actually, they never were good enough for that.

My boys are on the cusp of adulthood. They could be anything from here, go anywhere. It's all open to them. As a lover of possibilities, I'm glad for them. Possibilities feel like wealth to me, but I suppose they can be scary as well. I probably won't ever be a drug addict or an alcoholic, but I could have been. To do it now I would have to go at it with inten-tion and persistence, and it just seems like too much trouble.

I don't think I'm upset that I'll never be a pirate. I wanted to be one when I was a little girl. Scary and fierce, but in a nice way. That's a rough combination of qualities to master. I'm still trying.

I'm concerned that I'm living a cliché. I feel like every person in the English-speaking world, at least, goes through this chagrin at the closing down of possibilities in midlife. It's embarrassing. Then I have a terrible thought. Maybe what's next is the realization that there are still all kinds of possibilities out there, but most of them are bad: death, destruction, ruin, illness, loss. I remember talking to an eighty-two-year-old friend about the courage it takes to keep going when you never know what might be coming at you around the bend.

Here is what I'm going to do today. I'm going to be steeped in gratitude for what is now, for my health and for my friends, for my life as a landlubber, for my garden and the dogs and Mike the cat, for my life without Meryl.

The present moment is my wealth, and possibilities become irrelevant. No desire, no fear. I'll enjoy being here.

The Green After

❧

Today I have too many friends who are dying. Sometimes at a memorial service I feel dissatisfied, and I'm the preacher in charge. I realize I can't figure out how to preach my view of resurrection. I know that people would want to hear it, I'm not worried about offending or confusing anyone. I treasure the ability to speak the plain truth as I see it. The plain truth is no one knows for sure what happens when we die. That's not a very stirring thing to proclaim at a funeral, though, honest as it is. We all have some kind of belief about it, even if that belief is that there is nothing after we die. The reason I haven't preached it yet is because when I call to mind my belief about the afterlife, it comes to me as a color.

At a camping weekend with friends, we were nestled in a clearing on a mountainside. Most of the folks were around the campfire, talking or dozing. Our chef was in the cooking tent grilling and gossiping with his fiancée and a couple of others. He wasn't wearing his high heels that day. He does sometimes, but only on camping weekends. I love those people, and they love me. Being surrounded by love is one fine way to spend time. I wandered off to the hammock and lay there looking up at the sky through early April leaves. I was soaked with light, the blue of the sky, the green of young leaves, the sun shining through them like stained glass.

I thought, "When I die, I want to have my ashes buried under this tree, so that for one spring after another my body can be part of this particular green."

I could feel my life flowing through the cells of a leaf, feel the leaf opening to the warmth and the light, feel myself part of that green, and I was happy. If that is my afterlife, I will be deeply happy.

The hope of that afterlife doesn't take any leap of faith. I know it can happen. The minerals and the water in my body can be soaked up through the roots of that tree. A part of my body will unfurl, green in the sun.

My soul may be somewhere else. Sometimes I think my soul will float in an ocean of love. Will I recognize old friends, family who have gone on ahead? I don't know. I think I will know they are there. I will know this: There is not now nor was there ever any separation between us. I will know that they were with me the whole time, as strongly when I was alive as when I'm part of the leaves.

The green of a new leaf, lit from behind with the spring sun, stays inside me, a glowing place of peace, the certainty that I will always be part of life. During a memorial service I see that green, I feel that peace. It's hard to preach a color, but I'm going to think of a way.